Now I Know

YOU CAN'T
OUTGIVE
GOD

by

Jim Shifler

McDougal Publishing is a ministry of The
McDougal Foundation, Inc., a Maryland nonprofit
corporation dedicated to spreading the Gospel
of the Lord Jesus Christ to as many people
as possible in the shortest time possible.

Published by:

McDougal Publishing
P.O. Box 3595
Hagerstown, MD 21742-3595
www.mcdougalpublishing.com

ISBN 978-1-58158-158-4

Printed in the US, the UK and Australia
For Worldwide Distribution

Jim Shifler

DEDICATION

    This book is dedicated to the memory of two men who have been very influential in my life: my grandfather, Mr. Charles Easterday, and my dear friend and former Washington County Register of Wills, Mr. Harry A. Newcomer. These two men were my role models and my inspiration. They were examples of strong character and Christian values and blessed me with their friendship, their encouragement, and their love.

CONTENTS

INTRODUCTION

We've all heard the old saying, *"God moves in mysterious ways His wonders to perform."* I believe this saying is true, because I have experienced many of His mysterious ways over the eighty-five years of my life. For example, who would have thought that a boy born into a poor farm family and who grew up during the Great Depression would become one of the top Nationwide Insurance agents in the United States and be able to impact the lives of thousands of people? Who would have thought that God would bring an Englishman all the way back from China to ask that insurance agent a question that caused him to realize that he should write a book? Please allow me to explain:

In the Fall of 2008, my wife Ann's nephew, Gary Lee, phoned to say that he would like to spend a month with us. Gary and his wife, Mary, along with their two young sons, had traveled to China as missionaries with Agape, an organization associated with Campus Crusade for Christ International. During the preceding year, Gary had experienced three devastating losses. His mother, his father, who was Ann's brother Derrick, and his aunt, who was Ann's sister Audrey, had all passed away, resulting in an extremely painful time for Gary. He felt that our farm, located in the serene countryside of Maryland, would be an ideal place for him to relax and allow the Lord to minister comfort and peace to his troubled heart. So he called and asked if he could come there and spend some time with us. We were only too happy to oblige.

During his stay, Gary enjoyed walking for miles at a time on the country roads near our home. This gave him time to reflect and heal. Sometimes I would walk with him, and we would talk about the importance of our families, our faith, and our work. Besides my family and participation in my church, the most important thing in my life had been my twenty-eight-year career as an insurance agent. Gary was aware of the fact that, prior to my retirement, I had been one of the most successful agents in my company.

Maryland is beautiful in autumn, and as Gary and I walked down Garis Shop Road, we couldn't help admiring the magnificent splendor of the trees that lined it on both sides. A palette of scarlet, orange, and gold surrounded us. Even the ground was ablaze with a carpet of colorful leaves that had fallen from the trees and rustled beneath our feet as we walked. We were enjoying a relaxed conversation one day, when Gary suddenly looked at me and asked a question that had such depth and impact to it that it has caused me to ponder and meditate on its significance ever since. He said "Jim, how much credit have you given to God for being such a successful agent?" The question caught me off guard, and I couldn't give him a proper answer. Many times I had been asked to give talks to groups of other agents, sometimes to groups of more than a hundred at a time. I told them what my staff and I had done to sell so much insurance. I shared what I had been able to accomplish in fifteen years, with just my wife, Ruth, answering the telephone and typing policies (with the help of a part-time secretary). I had thirty-five hundred policies in force before I finally hired other agents to help me.

Now, a whole new perspective began to open up, as I looked back over my life and the many things that had happened to me. The more I thought about it, the more I realized just how instrumental God had been in leading me to my work and how He had blessed, prospered, and protected me, even sparing my life on at least two different occasions. Like many of us, I simply had never stopped to think about how He had orchestrated all these events that shaped my life.

Some time ago I heard a minister on television. He was telling how, when he was twelve years old, God had whispered to him that he should go to a church camp. Later, while attending college, God whispered to him again, this time that he should take a few courses in religion. This man had been planning to join his father's business, but shortly before he graduated, God again whispered to him, that he should go into the ministry. A few months later he started a church in a nightclub (that he could only use on Sundays). Today that man has one of the largest churches in a large American city.

In the Bible there are many instances of God speaking to people in dreams or visions or directly, such as when He spoke to Moses to lead the Israelites out of Egyptian bondage, or to Paul on the Road to Damascus. When He spoke to that minister, God opened doors for him that changed his life.

For the last three years, since Gary asked me that question, I have done a lot of thinking. As I looked back over my life, I began to realize that God had opened many doors for me. Those doors sometimes appeared in the guise of a person, a circumstance, or an opportunity, but once opened and walked through, each one carried with it a path and a plan. I began to experience an inner voice that kept saying, "You should write a book!" I found myself constantly thinking about this idea, but it wasn't something I particularly wanted to do. After much consideration, I decided to honor God and give Him glory for my success by sharing the story of my life in this book. I am surprised at how much I have been able to remember.

As you read these pages, I hope you will examine your own life, looking for the ways God has intervened and opened doors of blessing for you. You will probably be amazed at what you find.

Jim Shifler

CHAPTER ONE

HUMBLE BEGINNINGS

I have so many reasons to be thankful to the Lord. Out of all the millions of people on the earth, He gave me the wonderful opportunity to be born on a farm in the United States of America. I can't think of a better place for a young boy to grow up.

I was born on October 26, 1927, near the little town of Myersville, in the lush green mountains of Frederick County, Maryland. Our house was situated on a dirt road, and I was told that when the doctor came to deliver me he got stuck in the mud, and my father had to hitch the horses to his car and pull him out. The road was named Easterday Road, after my grandfather, a large, friendly man, well-liked by everyone, with snow-white hair (like mine). His name was Charles Easterday, and he and my grandmother Effie owned the farm where we lived and where my parents were tenant farmers (for my grandparents). This farm has been in the Easterday Family since 1775. It was a beautiful farm, with rolling hills and a big meadow, where the horses, cattle, and geese could graze, and with a stream running through it, where the animals could drink from the cool, refreshing water. My parents worked hard, milking the cows, tilling the fields, and doing all the other chores necessary to keep a busy farm going.

Early in my childhood, I was very sick with spinal meningitis — so sick that I nearly died. The doctor told my parents that he couldn't say which way it would go. Either I would improve and live, or I would die. I am thankful that the good Lord spared my life and healed me.

We often experienced very big snow storms when I was a young boy. I remember one winter when there was so much snow that the mailman delivered the mail with a horse-drawn sled. One Sunday, while we were at church (Myersville United Brethren, later to become Myersville United Methodist), there was such a big snow storm that we had a hard time getting back home. The winters were also a lot colder in those days than they are now. It was not unusual for temperatures to drop below zero.

My parents were Christians, so I was raised in the church and learned from an early age what it meant to love my neighbor and live by the Golden Rule. I had one sister and three brothers. My sister Elfleta was the oldest, followed by my older brother Seibert. Next was me, then my younger brother, Woodrow, and finally the youngest, our baby brother Charles.

I will never forget how my dad would handle the childhood fights and squabbles that sometimes erupted between us. He would make those of us involved in the altercation sit on a rail fence with our arms around each other. It was nearly impossible to stay mad, while balancing on a rail fence with your arms around your opponent. Thinking back, I can't honestly remember getting into fights with my sister and brothers after we moved to our next farm (which didn't have a rail fence). We may have been too busy to waste time fighting, because on the farm there was always a lot of work to do.

My mother said that when the picture on the next page was taken of the four of us (Charles wasn't born yet), my older

The Shifler siblings on a fence, about 1931

From the left: Myself, Seibert, Elfleta and Woody, about 1928

brother Seibert wouldn't smile. The photographer wanted to get him to smile, but he wouldn't do it, no matter what they tried. The photographer commented on the difference between us and how easily I smiled. The ability to keep a positive outlook on life and to keep on smiling is another of the gifts God has given me.

When I was about five years old, my parents did a very brave thing. It was during the Great Depression, and my mother was soon to give birth to her fifth child, baby brother Charles. In spite of these overwhelming obstacles, they decided to move to Washington County, Maryland, and go into farming for themselves. Because it was during the Depression and many of the banks had closed, it was nearly impossible to get a bank loan. My grandfather's sister, my Great-Aunt Laura Shifler, loaned my parents the money to buy the horses, cattle, and equipment they needed to get started. She was just a little woman, about five feet tall and weighing around a hundred pounds. I remember going along with my parents when they went to her house on Saturday nights to make the loan payments, and I recall that she was very nice.

We continued going to Aunt Laura's house and making those payments for many years, until the loan was eventually paid off. What my parents borrowed from her would have been a considerable amount for that time — about $2,000 to $3,000. Comparing that with what it costs to start farming today: a man recently bought a hundred cows and most, but not all, of the necessary machinery he would need, and he spent $1.2 million. How things have changed!

At that time, it was customary for the landowner and the tenant farmer to split the grain evenly, once it had been harvested. Today tenant farmers pay a certain amount per acre, depending on where the land is and how good it is, and then the entire crop belongs to them.

The Great Depression lasted for many years, and things continued to be difficult until the start of World War II. During those depression years, many banks failed. Our parents had started savings accounts for all of us children with money we received on our birthdays. Even though our bank didn't completely fail, when the time came, they were unable to return the amount deposited. Some years later, they paid us, but only pennies on the dollar for all of those accounts.

As a young boy, I remember walking across the field and down Mapleville Road to get to school. At that time, there were trolley tracks on that road. When we got a deep snow, my father would take my brother and me to school on horseback. Our school had six grades in one room and two other grades in a smaller building on the same property. There was no indoor plumbing in the school buildings, so we had to get our drinking water from a house next door. We all drank from the same cup. Of course, there were also no bathroom facilities, just an outhouse in back.

With six grades in one room, there were a lot of distractions, and it was easy for a small boy like me to get left in the dust. I only attended school there for two years, both of which were first grade, because I failed the first year and had to repeat it. Thinking back, I am not surprised that I failed. We had moved to Washington County in April, which was a major undertaking in itself, and then our brother Charles was born on May 26. So it was a rather hectic year.

Daddy and Mom did well at that first farm, and about two years later they received an offer to rent a larger farm, just over a mile away.

This second farm had the finest buildings of any farm I know of in the area, including a ten-room stone house that had outside walls that were about a foot and a half thick. Whenever you walked through an outside doorway, you could see the thickness of those walls. Other buildings on the farm included a barn, a wagon shed, a smokehouse (the only one in the area), a washhouse, a milk house, a chicken house and a two-car garage, although we never had more than one car and never owned a truck or a tractor. And there was one other building — the outside toilet.

Most importantly, this farm had a hundred and fifteen acres of tillable soil, with no waste ground at all. Most farms include rocky areas and wooded areas, which are not very beneficial to a farmer. This seemed like a great deal, and my parents decided to accept the offer. The owners of the land, Mr. and Mrs. Scott Doub, were the best landowners you could ever have found to deal with, and they remained friends with our family for many years to come.

So, the following spring we began the mammoth task of moving all the horses, cattle, and household articles to the new location. My sister Elfleta was twelve, Seibert was eight, I was seven, Woody was six, and little Charles was just two years old. From that time on, we attended school in Boonsboro.

At the Boonsboro School, all twelve grades were in the same building, and we enjoyed the luxury of indoor plumbing. There were separate classrooms, with a separate teacher, for each of the first six grades. My fifth-grade teacher was my favorite of the six teachers I had in elementary school. She told us that if we did our work well in class she would never give us homework, and she stuck to that promise. She was the only teacher I ever had who did that, and that's why she was my favorite.

I also remember another teacher in either third or fourth grade who really impressed me. On the first day of school she had us each introduce ourselves. Then she proceeded to go around the room and name each child from memory.

From the seventh grade and up, we had a different teacher for each subject. The school had a cafeteria, but Mom packed lunches for us.

The house and other buildings on our farm were just a little over four hundred feet from Route 40-A[1], also known as the National Pike, a road running west from Washington, D.C. (the first macadam road in this great country of ours). In our case, the road ran between Funkstown and Boonsboro,

---

1   Alternate Route 40 (ALT RT 40 or RT 40-A) is the nation's designation for portions of highway that were previously part of that famous route, usually through residential areas.

Maryland, and walking four hundred feet to catch the school bus was a lot easier than the mile-long walk we had made to the Mapleville School before.

The new farm was beautiful. Down our lane, there was a nice front yard, with two big maple trees that provided excellent shade in the summer and breathtaking colors in the fall. There was a door on the front of the house that opened into a large hallway, but we rarely used it. An older couple lived in four rooms on the other side of that hallway, so we usually used the back door.

When you came into our backyard, our milk house sat to the left. This milk house was about one hundred and fifty feet away from the barn. We children would take turns, getting up two one day and two the next, to milk the twelve dairy cows. Of course we milked them by hand, and this had to be done twice a day, once in the early morning and once in the evening, 365 days a year. To make the work go faster, we used to play a game to see how far we could squirt the milk. Of course, the cats loved this game and would hang around to get a warm, tasty treat.

After milking the cows we carried the milk up to the milk house in buckets, strained it to remove any dirt, and poured it into ten-gallon cans. Those cans weighed about eighty-five pounds when full, which was a lot of lifting and tugging.

To keep the milk from spoiling, we then placed the milk cans into a concrete watering trough filled with cold water. There was a well in the milk house, with an electric pump, to supply water to two watering troughs, one to water the livestock, and the other to cool the milk cans until the milk truck came by each day, to haul it to the processing plant.

We also got our drinking water from that well. On the right, we had a hand pump for a cistern. We used that water, which came off the house roof when it rained, for baths and for washing dishes and clothes. Today such cisterns have been outlawed.

A few years later, we built a new milk house down next to the barn. We also had a water line run down there from the well, and we put in a milk cooler. These improvements made our work a whole lot easier.

Back in those days, when we got a big rain, the water would run across Route 40-A and down our lane. One time it rained so hard that an unbelievable amount of water rushed into our barnyard, and something very unusual occurred. There's an area just beside our milk house that's sort of downhill. The water started eroding the soil and making a hole in the ground there beside the water trough. This hole started out small, but little by little, it got deeper and wider ... until it was so big you could bury a horse in it. I haven't seen water come across the highway like that for many years now, because the water table has gone down. Due to the lower water table, the original well that we used for all our drinking water eventually went dry, and it was necessary to drill a deeper well at a new location.

From the original milk house, it was only a few steps to our back porch, where we had a closet built into the outside wall. In that area, there was a place to wash our hands and an oil-burning stove that we used for cooking in the summertime, when the weather was warm. There was also a large wooden box to store the wood used for the cook stove in the kitchen. This stove sat on the right as you entered the kitchen, and it had a water tank on one end that supplied all the hot water that we used in the house. There was also a dry sink.[2]

We had no refrigerator to keep our food from spoiling, just an icebox. Ice would be delivered periodically to the house for this purpose. We had a kitchen cabinet where we kept spices and other items that were needed for preparing food. There was a big table that would seat eight people, three on a long bench and the others on separate chairs.

The house had two basements that could be entered from either inside or outside. There we stored potatoes, canned fruit and vegetables, a barrel of vinegar, and a barrel of cider. We grew apples in our own orchard and took them to the cider press in the fall, where they were made into cider.

There was also an attic at each end of the house. In the winter we sometimes made ice cream in the basement, using the ice that froze in the watering trough and an old hand-operated ice cream churn. I can still remember how delicious that ice cream was.

---

2   For those who are unfamiliar with a dry sink, this was a cabinet used for washing before indoor plumbing became popular. Dry sinks can still be found for sale, but they are mostly used now for decoration rather than personal hygiene.

You Can't Outgive God

Besides the cook stove in the kitchen, the only other heat in the house was a parlor stove in the living room that burned coal. This would burn twenty-four hours a day in the winter. In the ceiling above this stove were vents, which allowed some of the heat to rise to the second floor, to heat the bedrooms. Four of us slept in the same room upstairs, in two double beds. One of the four was a hired hand. The others were my two brothers and myself.

The fire in the cook stove would go out at night. When my father got up early in the morning, the first thing he did was light his pipe. Then he went out on the porch and got some wood and started a fire in the cook stove, so my mother could cook breakfast. The cows had to be milked, the livestock fed, and the stable cleaned out before we could eat breakfast.

There was too much hard work on the farm for my father to do it all, and so until my brothers and I were old enough to be of more use to him, we had a hired hand who lived in the house with us, and we gave him all his meals. He had been our neighbor on the farm where I was born in Frederick County. He only worked for us about seven months a year; we didn't need his help in the wintertime.

The two fields along Route 40-A in front of our house were very level and didn't have a lot of rocks. One day a man stopped in to ask if he could take off and land his airplane in those fields. Daddy agreed, and the man did this for a number of years ... until his plane hit the wire fence between the two fields. After that, he didn't land there anymore.

We children learned to do small jobs on the farm from the time we were very young. We carried wood in for the wood box, picked up potatoes in the field, and otherwise worked in the garden, learning how to plant both seeds and plants. Many years later I had the opportunity to watch an engineer planting a garden for the first time. I had to laugh when I saw him planting seeds. He was using a tape measure to space the seeds and to see how deep to plant them, making sure he was doing it just right. The children in our family had done this so many times that we knew exactly how far apart and how deep to plant all kinds of seeds. We didn't need a tape measure.

Another job we did, as young boys, was picking black raspberries for a neighbor. He would come get us very early in the morning, and we would pick for half a day or more, depending on the quantity of the berries available that season. When we were done picking, the neighbor would take us home. At the time, we received 1 ¼ cents per quart for picking raspberries. This was later raised to 3 cents a quart. My brother grows raspberries, and he now pays $1 a quart to those who pick them. How times have changed!

Not long after we moved to the second farm, I remember how much I enjoyed going back over to my grandparents' home, where I was born and lived during the early years of my life. I would stay with them for several weeks at a time. During my stay, I did small chores, like helping my grandmother in the garden. My grandfather sent me to the meadow to cut milk weeds with a corn chopper. He gave me a quarter or 50 cents for doing this. I also helped my grandparents separate milk and churn it into butter. On Saturday, we went to town to deliver goods from the farm. One day, when we were on our way to town, the wheel came off of the car. I was in the back seat with the eggs, and they went everywhere. What a mess!

My grandparents' house had no electricity, and they got their drinking water from a spring in the meadow. There was a hand pump that pushed water into the house. They kept a small pail of water by that pump, because, most of the time, you had to prime it before you could get any water from it. We had to pour water into the top of the pump to remove the air before the pump could bring forth a flow of water.

My grandmother often fixed two of my favorite foods, a big goose egg, or her very delicious fried potatoes. I can still remember how good they tasted. Another treat I recall was when my grandfather would take me to the local picnics and buy me all the ice cream I wanted. That was the only ice cream I ever got, except for the homemade kind our family made in the wintertime. I love ice cream, so I really enjoyed that.

My grandparents didn't sell their milk. They separated it and made it into butter and gave the milk that was left to the hogs. They raised huge Poland China Hogs, some of them weighing eight hundred to a thousand pounds each. I was talking to my first cousin recently, and he said he can still remember me carrying buckets of milk to the spring house on my grandparents' farm.

The men and boys worked hard on the farm, but so did my mother. She cooked three meals a day, including a large breakfast, because a lot of our work had to be done in the mornings. Breakfast usually included fried potatoes, hominy, pudding,[3] and eggs. We had to get up very early to get the milking done, feed the horses, and then eat a big breakfast before leaving for school.

Mother made all of our breads, rolls, potpies, and all kinds of fruit pies — including mock mince pie, crumb pie, sweet potato pie, green tomato pie, and the normal varieties of fruit pies. She was a good cook and a fast one. Her ham-bean potpie was the best potpie I have ever eaten. The ham was from hogs we had raised and butchered ourselves and had smoked in the smokehouse on our own farm.

Mom did so much baking that she bought flour by the fifty-pound bag. It was stored in a flour chest in the wash house. In those days flour came in bags made of attractive printed muslin, and women sometimes used this cloth to make dresses and aprons. Today we buy a five-pound bag of flour, and it takes quite a while for us to use it all.

My mother took care of all the bookkeeping for the farm and, in later years, she also worked in the garden. In addition to the garden, we had a truck patch, where we grew rows of potatoes, sweet potatoes, and sweet corn. She roasted the sweet corn and cut it off the cob, and we put it on the tin roof of the chicken house to dry.

---

3   This was meat pudding, not sweet pudding.

You Can't Outgive God

My sister Elfleta was a big help to my mother with all the household chores. I still remember how upset Elfleta got when we walked across her freshly-washed floors with our dirty shoes. Many years later, my brothers and I still liked to kid her about that.

We raised hogs and chickens. In the springtime, we would go into Hagerstown and buy about a hundred peeps that were already hatched, take them home, and raise them into grown chickens. We had to keep a light on the peeps twenty-four hours a day to keep them warm. People were known to steal chickens in those days, so my father hooked up a burglar alarm system that would sound if someone opened the door to the chicken house. When my mother wanted to fix chicken for dinner, she would kill and clean the chickens herself and singe them over the woodstove. There's nothing quite like a fresh chicken dinner with all the trimmings.

We had a washhouse with a fireplace. To wash clothes, we built a fire in the fireplace, pumped the water from the cistern, and heated it in two big kettles. We had a Maytag wringer washer, which had to be filled with water by hand. After the clothes were washed, they were put through the wringer and then into a big wash pan of water to rinse them. Then they had to be put through the wringer again to get the excess rinse water out. Of course there were no electric dryers in those days, so my mother hung all the clothes on the clothesline to dry.

Daddy also used the washhouse as a workshop. That's where he cut our hair and repaired our shoes. With such a large family, he saved a lot of money over the years by doing those things himself.

The washhouse had a second floor that we kids used as a playhouse. This building and the barn both had tin roofs, and I will never forget the soothing and relaxing sound of rain hitting on a tin roof. It's a sound like no other. So many people today miss out on this, but we were blessed to get to hear it often, and we enjoyed it.

On Saturday evenings, our family went into town, to shop for groceries (and to stop at Aunt Laura's house to make a payment on that loan). I was receiving an allowance each week of a nickel, and there was a little store across the street from Aunt Laura's house where they sold candy, cracker jacks, and other treats. I remember going to that store and how carefully I searched for the perfect item to purchase with my precious nickel.

Another thing I remember from my childhood was the kinds of clothes we wore. Being from a large family, I wore a lot of hand-me-downs that had previously belonged to my older brother, Seibert. When I outgrew them, they were then passed along to Woody. Charles was a lot younger, and there probably wasn't much left of those clothes by the time he could wear them, so he usually got something new.

One item of clothing I hated was knee pants. They had elastic, to keep them up at the knee, but as the elastic wore out, they would work their way down your legs. That was very uncomfortable!

We never had many toys, so we had to use our imaginations. We made a sling-shot out of an old inner tube or a bow and arrow using twigs from the trees. One of us used to get inside of an old tire, and the others would push the tire and roll him around. We also made a swing with a tire. Sometimes neighbors came over, and we played softball in our field.

Woody and I had bicycles, and we rode them a lot. One day I was taking my brother Charles for a ride on the bike, and he was sitting on the handlebars. There were rubber grips on the handlebars for me to hold on to, and that day, suddenly, while I was standing up peddling, one of those grips came off, and I lost control of the bike. I darted right into traffic, and a car hit us. This could have resulted in a terrible tragedy, but God was looking out for us, and neither of us was badly injured.

In the summertimes, my brothers and I enjoyed spending time at Beaver Creek near our farm. We would dam up the water and make an area where it was deep enough to swim. When it was hot and we had done some dirty chores on the farm, instead of taking a bath, we got on our bicycles and rode over and jumped in the creek. That cold water felt so good after long hours of working in the hot sun.

I remember one Christmas when we three older boys got a football. This was our main gift, and we had to share it between the three of us. Other than that, all we got was an orange and some candy for each of us. We started throwing the football around in the house at about four o'clock on Christmas morning and broke one of my mother's vases. Needless to say, that ended our football playing in the house.

I enjoyed competition and, as a boy, I liked to make up games in which I competed with myself or sometimes with other people. I tried to figure out the fastest way of doing things. I had learned that no matter how many times you have done something, you might still find another better or faster way of doing it. I was always looking for a shortcut that would be more efficient and save time. This later helped me when I played basketball and soccer, and also in my chosen career.

Something that happened when I was a freshman at Boonsboro High School taught me a very important principle, one that has stuck with me throughout life. At our school, you had to be at least a freshman before you were allowed to play in the gym. I can still remember how excited I was when I had my first opportunity to shoot baskets there.

I found the thrill of the ball swishing through the hoop to be wonderful, and a dream was birthed within me that day to become a good basketball player and to be on the varsity team. Usually it was the tall guys who went out for basketball, and I was very short. At the time, I was only about five feet six inches tall, but I decided not to let that stop me. What I lacked in height I made up for with desire, determination, and devotion.

To get better at the game, I didn't have money to buy a basketball or a net, so I used what I had — my imagination. When I got back to the farm, I took the bottom out of a half-bushel basket and nailed it to the side of our big wagon shed. There was no grass in the barnyard, and the ground was packed solid because the horses and cows were in there all the time. For a ball, I also used what I had. It was a soccer ball, and it was much lighter than a basketball, but I began practicing with that.

The type of homemade basketball hoop I practiced with

I spent many hours learning to dribble the ball and then to make two-handed shots. Then one day I tried something new. I began to shoot a different kind of shot, one that would be harder for my opponents to block — a hook shot. Some people thought this wasn't very practical, but it turned out to be an important breakthrough for me.

I continued to put in long hours, perfecting this shot, along with my other basketball skills, all during my freshman year and throughout the following summer. When I became a sophomore, I tried out for the varsity team, and was over-whelmed with joy when I made it. I was the only sophomore on the team, and it was my hook shot that had given me the edge I needed. I went on to play on the varsity team in my sophomore, junior, and senior years. My brothers, Seibert and Woody, also played basketball.

When I was a senior, I was selected to be the team captain and was also the top scorer. Looking back on our team picture that year, there I am, standing in the middle of the front row, the captain of the team and one of the shortest guys in the picture. My many hours spent in the barnyard practicing had definitely paid off.

I had learned a very important principle, one that has stuck with me and been a pillar of my success. I call it the three D's: Desire, Determination, and Devotion. This secret will work for anyone who will put it into practice. When you want to do something, there is a way to get it done. But first, you must lay aside all excuses and obstacles. People often make excuses, but the real reason they don't follow their dreams and find success is that they don't try hard enough. If your desire, your determination, and your devotion are strong, you will be amazed at what you can accomplish. I have used this principle over and over again in life, and it has never failed me.

I was also co-captain of the soccer team in my senior year, and when we had Field Day, I was on the relay team. I got straight A's in sports, but I made a lot of B's and C's (I can only remember one D) in other subjects, maintaining about a C+ average. Obviously, I didn't apply myself as well as I should have, but there was another factor. Looking back at my report card from my senior year, I noticed that my father had taken me out of school eight days because he needed my help on the farm. The farm always took priority in those days.

I remember some of my high school teachers. There was one who had a habit of flicking students on the ear with his index finger just to get their attention. We had a math teacher who liked to talk. If we could get him started on some subject, he would talk about it the whole class period, and never get around to teaching math. Of course we always tried to get him to do this, so we could avoid math. We also had a male teacher who liked the girls. He was a sharp dresser and would seat the prettiest girls right up next to his desk.

I definitely remember our Industrial Arts teacher. He had each of us students pick out something we would like to make. Then, when the project was part-way completed, he would examine it, and if he liked it he simply set it back down. If he didn't like it, he would throw it across the room. At the time, I thought this was funny, but today a teacher probably wouldn't get away with exhibiting this type of behavior in the classroom. That teacher lived next door to us, and was still alive well into his nineties.

When I was a sophomore, my English teacher gave our class a special assignment. We were each to write the biography of someone we knew very well. I chose to write about my grandfather, Charles Easterday, and I would like to share that essay with you here:

BIOGRAPHY OF CHARLES EASTERDAY
WRITTEN BY JAMES E. SHIFLER
December, 1944

We were asked to write a biography of someone we know very well. This set me to thinking of some people I know or knew. This meant I should have a deep and sound knowledge of the person whose life story you write about. Well, I finally decided that my grandfather was one of the most out-standing men I ever knew or hope to know. I know I can't make it near so interesting as some great writer, but I'll try to do my best. In the year 1873, on a farm near Myers-ville, a boy was born. It was on June 6th, a beautiful summer day, making a person feel like going swimming or sitting under a shade tree, taking it easy. He was the first child and, of course, his parents were very proud of their newborn son. Little did people know what kind of man he was to become.

He started to school when he was six years old. He just had to go across the fields to school. There were no ways of going to school except to walk. When he was a young boy, his father used to make him ride a horse to a nearby town. He said that he used to pity the horse and get off and walk. He used to laugh about it, after he would finish telling it.

When he finished elementary school, which was only seven grades, he came to Boonsboro High. He would walk over to school on Monday morning and stay with his aunt in Boonsboro at night. When Friday came he wouldn't run out to get on a bus or car, but he would walk the ten miles home, over the winding road.

He had to go to school from September to May, which is a shorter school year than we have today. The road soon became very familiar to him, and he could almost walk over it with his eyes closed. In 1889, he graduated from high school.

He was a very intelligent man; just could of taught school, but he refused and, instead, went to farming with his brother, sister, and mother.

My grandfather learned to play about six musical instruments. He played the coronet in the Myersville Band, and this was the way he met his wife. The band played in a town near Baltimore, and my grandmother happened to be there, too, with her boyfriend. They all sat at one table to have lunch. When they finished their lunch, all got up, except my grandparents. About a year later, they were married in Myersville and had their honeymoon in the historic town of Sharpsburg.

In 1902, my grandfather built a house on his farm, and the same year my mother was born. She grew up very fast (time slips away), and before long, she was married.

A few days after I was born, my grandfather's barn burned down. They spent the whole winter cutting timber off his farm, and, with the aid of his neighbors, he soon had the barn rebuilt.

When I was five, we moved from his place to a farm near Boonsboro. After that, in the summers, my two brothers and I spent our vacation at his farm.

Then, last June, after his seventy-first birthday, my grandfather died from a fall. It was a shock to the whole community that such a healthy man as my grandfather should die so suddenly. He was a man about 6 feet 7 inches tall, with his weight over 200 pounds. One of the reasons he was so healthy was that he never smoked, drank, or used the Lord's name in vain.

He also drank a half gallon of milk every night. Then he would read the paper before going to sleep, waking up, reading some more, and finally he would go to bed.

He had some hobbies, not like most people: hunting, fishing, going to movies, or listening to the radio. They were very different: like planting trees, especially fruit trees. He also kept a scrapbook containing different things, such as pictures, poetry, letters, and his pride of all was the things he wrote himself. The best thing he liked on the farm was raising hogs.

One of my grandmother's hobbies was raising chickens to eat. She never made any money off them, instead loss. My grandfather never said anything about it, because it made her happy. He would never say anything unkind to anyone or be angry with anybody. He always had kind of a smile, yet he was quite serious.

Well, you see that my grandfather was not much different than some person you know. Just stop and think of some person you like very dearly and see what kind of biography you can write. Truly I think he was a great man in the eyes of other people, a man who loved his family, his country, and his God.

Hoping to live up to the standard he set, I remain his grandson, James Shifler.

Written by James E. Shifler
Grandson of Charles Easterday,
and Son of Mr. & Mrs. Shirley Shifler,
of Boonsboro, Maryland

Another thing I did in high school that I really enjoyed was acting in the Senior Class play. I never dreamed I could do something like that. I remembered the trouble I'd had saying one-line recitations during programs at church. I guess I

As Tate Smithers in my Senior Class play

hadn't worked hard enough at learning them. In the Senior play, I had seventy different speaking parts. It was a comedy called "Double Exposure," and I had the part of Tate Smithers, the county constable (See the photo on the previous page). After the play, an article in the Boonsboro newspaper said that I had "brought the house down." When I graduated and walked across the stage to get my diploma, I heard the lady who convinced me to take the part in the play say, "There goes Tate Smithers."

I have a lot of fond memories from high school. I also enjoyed singing in the glee club. In looking through the 1946 Boonsboro High School Yearbook, I noticed that I was selected as the boy in our graduating class with the "prettiest eyes."

When I was in high school, I often had to stay late to practice basketball, soccer, or for the Senior Class play. Since the buses had stopped running for the day by the time I was ready to go home, I would usually thumb a ride. Hitchhiking was a common practice in those days, and the people who picked me up were friendly and were glad to offer me a ride.

My sister Elfleta had dated a neighbor boy named Ellsworth Reeder, and they were married in 1944. Ellsworth's father decided to make his living as a carpenter, and he and his wife went to live in Boonsboro, turning the farm over to Ellsworth and Elfleta.

Once, before I went into the Navy, I borrowed Ellsworth's car to go on a date with a girl down in Rohrersville. I parked the car on a hill and went into her house. Before long someone came rushing in and said, "A car's running down the road!" I dashed out of the house and looked, and it was mine (or, rather, my brother-in-law's). I ran down to see what had happened, and was amazed with what I found. There was a pine tree on one side of the car and a house on the other, with only three or four feet to spare. The car had backed right in between them, and, to my relief, it didn't have a scratch on it. Wow!

CHAPTER TWO

A LEGACY OF HARD WORK

Most Americans have seen pictures of the early settlers who came to this country and know something about how they lived and how difficult their lives were. I thought it might be interesting for you to know how hard we worked when I was a boy living on the farm. It was a good life, but certainly not an easy one. At that time, farming was all done with horses and wagons, which was a lot of hard, backbreaking work.

One day, when my brother Woody and I were about eleven and twelve, Daddy told us to go out to plow a certain field. The field he sent us to turned out to be one of the rockiest places on the whole farm. We have often tried to figure out if he did that on purpose or not. Whatever the case, the rocks made it a much more difficult field to plow.

To accomplish what our father was asking of us, we first had to hitch up a team of three horses to a bar-shear plow. That plow was made of wood and had handles on each side. It had an odd-shaped metal blade that turned over eighteen inches of soil at a time, going about eight inches deep. The plow weighed sixty or seventy pounds, so this was very hard work for a twelve-year-old.

You Can't Outgive God

The horses pulled the plow, but I had to walk behind it, making sure the blade stayed in the ground and turned the soil over. My brother rode the lead horse, which helped, because I didn't have to be concerned about where the horses were going. When I hit a rock, which was quite often in that field, the plow would either jump up out of the ground, get stuck, or fall over. Then I had to stop the horses, straighten up the plow, and start over. I didn't have to actually lift the whole plow, but I had to get it upright.

At the end of each row, I had to throw the plow over, and it drug on the ground while the horses turned. This space on the end of the rows where the horses turned was called a "headland." Then I had to upright the plow again and start the next row. We would go back and plow the headland after we had finished the rest of the field. This was a man's work, but it was what Daddy expected of us, and we did our best to meet his expectations. Woody and I still talk about that.

We would soon learn to do many other difficult farm jobs. As we grew, we graduated from one task to the next.

The most important building on the farm, other than the house, was the big two-story bank barn, which was about seventy feet long, forty feet wide and forty feet high. My favorite thing about living on the farm was being around that barn and all the things that happened there. I have traveled all over the United States and, to my surprise, I have found that only Maryland and Pennsylvania have this attractive type of barn. I have seen a few in other states, but most of them were not well maintained. In some places, there are no barns, and the farming equipment is left sitting out in the fields.

A lot of thought went into the design of this particular barn. Someone with a good mind and a thorough understanding of farming methods did a wonderful job planning it. The way the barn was constructed made it perfect for housing the horses and cows and for storing the grain and hay we grew. Amazingly, that original barn is still standing and in good condition today. It was built before the Civil War, so it is well over two hundred years old.

There is a big iron bar beside the stable door, where the horses were kept. This bar was used to secure the door and prevent people from stealing horses during the war. Although this type of barn was practical for hundreds of years, this is no longer the case. The farmers of today either no longer have horses or milk cows, or they have too many milk cows for such a barn to be practical.

There is a picture of this barn on the next page. As you look at the barn, you will see that there is a forebay that extends out about nine feet from the main part of the barn. The cows used to go under there to keep out of the rain, but it also had other functions. When we threshed wheat, we would back the truck under the forebay and put bags of grain down through a hole in the barn floor, to load them directly into the bed of the truck, so that we could take the grain to the mill. When we were loading the manure

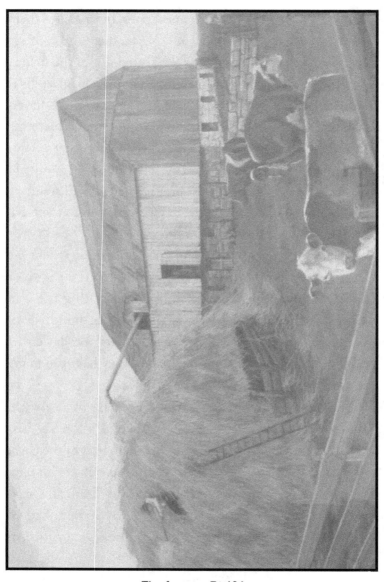

The farm on Rt 40A
A painting of the barn and the straw stack during threshing

spreader, we pulled it in under the forebay about a foot from the door of the stable and pitched the manure right into the spreader. We would also do this, if it was raining, to keep from getting wet.

Under the forebay were six doors which opened into six stables. Since we had six horses and a dozen milk cows, plus a number of heifers, we raised several different crops to provide food for all of them. Raising corn took longer than any other crop. We started in the spring by spreading the manure we had cleaned out of the stables and stored in the barnyard over the winter.

To provide bedding for the animals, we used a straw fork to pull the straw down from the stack. The straw fork looked like a fork with the teeth turned up, forming a hook. Then we used a regular four-pronged fork to carry the straw into the stable. This was different from a pitch fork, which had only two prongs and a longer handle and was used to pitch wheat or hay. When we cleaned the stables, we carried the straw and manure out, again using a four-pronged fork. Just think how much work this involved! First we carried the straw in, fork-by-fork, and then we carried all the manure out, fork-by-fork. Over the course of a year, we had carried that whole straw stack into the stable.

The manure was loaded into a spreader, which was pulled by two horses. Imagine loading enough manure to cover twenty-five acres of field, again using just a hand fork. That's what we had to do to load the manure spreader. This was the first step in planting corn.

The next step was to plow the fields. This was done using the same bar-shear plow I described earlier. We plowed twenty-five acres, which would take us weeks. In those days, a team of three horses and the plow cost us around $250. Today this same job is done using a tractor, which costs $100,000, and a plow, which costs about $25,000. With this equipment, farmers can now plow about eight acres an hour.

Once the fields were plowed, we had to harrow them. The harrow was a piece of equipment about nine feet wide by four feet. It had approximately a dozen teeth and was pulled by three horses. The harrow would pull up any big clumps of dirt and large stones. We could either walk beside the harrow or ride on the lead horse. When we walked behind a plow, we could lean on the plow, but with the harrow we were walking on soft dirt all day, and that was very difficult and tiring. Sometimes I rode the lead horse, but then, like my grandfather, I would feel sorry for the horse (because he was doing two jobs), and I didn't feel as if I was doing anything.

Next, we would take a wagon out and pick up by hand any large rocks that had come to the surface, put them in the wagon, and haul them to a rock pile somewhere on the farm. It was amazing that no matter how many times we had plowed and harrowed a field, we kept digging out more rocks each time.

Now the fields were ready, and we could plant the corn. As we planted the corn, we would look for a part of the field that had especially good soil, and that was where we planted our pumpkin seeds. Mom would use the resulting pumpkins to make delicious pies in the fall.

After the corn had come up, usually in June, we would plow to get the weeds out, working in the same direction that we had originally planted the field. A few weeks later, we plowed in the other direction, to get out the weeds that grew between the rows of corn. Then we plowed a third time, going back the same way as the first time. As you can see, this was a whole lot of work. When I was talking to Woody recently, he reminded me that one day, when we were plowing corn to get the weeds out, each with a team of horses and a plow, a neighbor saw us racing to see who could plow the fastest. That next Sunday, at church, this neighbor told our father what we had done, and Daddy wasn't very happy with us. Plowing was serious business.

By the middle of August, we could start cutting corn. A hill of corn contained one to three stalks, and each stalk had an ear of corn on it, which made it heavy to carry, probably about thirty pounds. To protect our arms from the corn, we would wear a sleeve made from an old pants leg (as shown in the photo on the next page). We made a hole in the sleeve for our thumb and put a string at the other end of the sleeve to tie around our chest, to keep the sleeve from sliding off. In addition to this, we had to wear long pants and a long-sleeved shirt. Since we were working in the hot days of late summer, August and September, this could be

Me dressed to cut corn.

VIEW OF BLOODY LANE AND BATTLEFIELD FROM OBSERVATION TOWER, ANTIETAM, MD.

A cornfield showing the pattern of uniform shocks of corn

very uncomfortable.

Cutting corn took hours of hard work in the hot sun, and you can understand how exhausting this would be, but when we were done, the reward for our labor was a very orderly and attractive field. People today never get to see the shocks of corn standing in the fields, because it is no longer done that way. Even most of those who have seen it sometime in the past have no idea how the shocks got that way.

With three growing boys in the family, Daddy now had

We used a corn chopper like this to cut 25 acres of corn.

plenty of help, so he often let us work for neighboring farmers as well. When I was about fourteen or fifteen, he told our neighbor that Woody and I would help him cut corn. When we got to that neighbor's farm in the morning, he commented, "I can't believe your father sent me two boys to cut corn with four grown men!" Woody and I set to work with the men. At mid-morning, we stopped to take a break and all drank from the same wooden keg. What amazed me most was that, instead of sitting down to rest, some of the men chose to remain on their feet. I was surprised that they didn't sit down on the ground.

At noon we stopped for lunch, and in the middle of the afternoon we got another break. Again, the men did not sit down to rest during their break.

When Woody and I finished what they had asked us to do, the other men were still cutting and gathering the rest of the corn, so we went and helped them. Our neighbor couldn't believe that we young boys had worked all day and kept up with grown men. Hard work was no stranger to us.

Daddy never paid us for working on our own farm, but when we went to work for a neighboring farmer, he told us we could keep the money we earned. As I noted earlier, Mom always packed our lunches for school, and I had never liked that. Most of the other parents gave their children money to buy lunches in the school cafeteria. A good lunch would cost just 25 cents. So, when I had worked and earned my own money, I would use it to buy lunch at school. I was earning

$4 a day; that was enough to buy me sixteen lunches.

Growing corn is very different today, and a whole lot less work. Now farmers no longer actually plant corn. Instead, it is sown, and the rows are much closer together. We always spread manure on the fields first, but today chemical fertilizers are also used. Farmers today don't plow for weeds. Instead they wait until the corn comes up, and then they spray the ground with weed killer. The result is that they never have a weed to deal with. Instead of using a corn chopper to cut the corn, they now use a machine called a "combine," which costs $400,000. This piece of equipment cuts and shells the corn and is able to do six acres in a single hour. What would have taken us months to do can now be accomplished in a single day. How times have changed!

When we finished cutting corn in September, we got ready to plant winter wheat or barley in the same field because the soil improved with the rotation of crops. When Ann and I traveled out West to Montana, we learned that the farmers there let a field rest for a whole year and only plant it every second year.

To prepare the field for planting wheat, we first used a big disc about nine feet wide and five feet long. This was pulled by three horses. This disc would remove the corn stalks by chopping them up and mixing them with the soil. We used the disc on the whole twenty-five acres and then took the harrow, also pulled by three horses, over the field. We had to walk behind both the disc and the harrow, which was a lot of walking. The work took several days, and it was very difficult to walk on loose ground. Again, the amount of hard work we did was almost unbelievable. Only after all of this was done did we plant the wheat or barley.

If we wanted to plant timothy hay, we did that at the same time, and the two crops would come up together. These grains were planted with a drill that had three compartments: one for the wheat or barley, one for the timothy, and one for the fertilizer. This apparatus was pulled by two horses, and we also had to walk behind it.

Instead of the timothy hay, sometimes we chose to plant clover, which also produced a type of hay. One planting of clover would usually produce hay for a couple of years. The clover was planted while the wheat was in the field, but not at the same time. We planted clover around the first of March, when the ground was freezing and thawing. To plant the clover, we used a device that looked like a small bag with a handle to crank. The bag had a strap that fit around your neck. A bag full of clover seeds weighed about fifteen pounds. The seeds would fall on the ground and into the cracks made by the freezing and thawing, and this was the desired method for planting it. The fact that it worked has always been a mystery to me.

The wheat was harvested before the clover hay, but this didn't disturb the clover at all. Around the last of June or first of July we harvested the wheat or barley. I always enjoyed driving by these fields when they were ready for harvesting.

You Can't Outgive God

They were golden and beautiful. Watching the stalks of grain blow in the wind was a sight to behold. Today few farmers in our area plant these grains. Most plant soybeans and corn, because livestock do better on them, and now milk production is the name of the game.

How did we harvest the grain in those days? We cut it with what was called a binder, which was pulled by five horses. It took a lot of time to harness five horses and get them ready to pull a binder. The binder would form the wheat into a sheaf, using binder twine, and then tie it with a tight knot. The person riding the binder watched for rocks in the field, and if there was a rock in the way, he would raise the platform of the binder to avoid hitting it.

Daddy often asked Mom to be the one who rode the binder. Can you imagine him doing that? I always felt it was wrong for him to expect her to do this, when it was a job that one of us kids could have been doing. She already had plenty to keep her occupied, cooking three meals a day, washing all our clothes with that old wringer washer, drying them on the clothesline, and then ironing all the clothes. She also worked in the garden and canned fruit and vegetables, dried corn, and did all the bookkeeping for the farm. Doing all of that and taking care of five kids was a LOT of work, but Daddy still wanted her to be the one to ride the binder, and so she would do it.

Once the wheat was ripe, it was important to get it into the barn as soon as possible. The longer it was out in the field the more chance it had of getting wet when it rained. The wheat had to be totally dry when we put it in the mow, because of the danger of combustion, which could set the barn on fire.

Once a neighbor asked my father to help him haul in his wheat, and so we took our wagon, hitched to two of our horses and went there to help. Daddy drove the wagon while Seibert and I loaded the grain. But there was a problem. On our farm, we didn't have steep hills, but this farm did, and Daddy was afraid that if he turned the wagon too sharply, it could upset. We loaded the wagon about half full and were going down one of those hills to get some more shocks of wheat. To keep the wagon from upsetting, he had to approach the hill on a slant and go down gradually.

What happened next I was never sure. It's possible that because we were on a slant some of the wheat was hanging over the side of the wagon and caused it to upset. Whatever the reason, the entire load was dumped out, and we had to get down and reload it all. The wheat was unharmed, and no one was physically injured, but it sure hurt our pride to have that happen when we were helping a neighbor.

Once the wheat was in the barn, we were ready to thresh the grain. A man who owned a threshing machine would charge us to use it. It came with a very big steam engine. We would open the sliding doors on the barn, and he would unhook the threshing machine from the steam engine, turn the steam engine around, and push the threshing machine into the barn, getting it as close as possible to the front of the barn so it was in position to blow the straw out onto our straw stack.

The owner of the machine worked the blower that directed where the straw was to go on the stack. The straw came flying out of a round pipe onto the stack outside. Another man was positioned on the straw stack to make sure the straw was evenly stacked. I did that job a couple times, as an older teen. It paid $5 a day, a dollar a day more than the other jobs. On page 44 is a picture of our straw stack, which is something no one has seen now for many years. Having enough straw was very important to farmers in our era.

Stacking the straw was the dustiest job, but working in the hay mow, throwing down the sheaves of wheat, was the hottest. Can you imagine working in that hay mow for three or four hours in ninety-degree temperatures? One man had to walk to the back of the hay mow, get a sheaf of wheat, and throw it out to a second man. There was no air circulating up there, and the heat from the threshing machine added to the discomfort.

Once we started the threshing machine, we never stopped for anything until lunchtime ... unless the machine broke down. I actually used to wish it *would* break down, so we could take a rest. Later, when I got my job as an insurance agent, it was so much easier than our work on the farm that I remember asking myself, "How did I get such an easy job?" I hadn't asked for it, but God was watching out for me.

Even though life on the farm was hard, I often think back to those days. It's a shame to think that we don't have a binder anymore to make those pretty shocks of wheat in the field, and that there are no horses plowing in the fields. I'm glad I was part of this history and got to see all of this happening.

The man who ran the steam engine, when we threshed wheat, was a neighbor who lived not too far from us. He used to pay me to walk up to his farm and milk his cow. One day I overheard him speaking with another man, and he made a humorous comment. They were talking about a fellow who hadn't been able to find a girl to marry, and his observation was, "Well, there's a lid for every pot." I have never forgotten those words.

I'm sure you have heard the saying, *"Make hay while the sun shines."* This saying works, not only for making hay, but for any job that needs to get done. Instead of procrastinating, you need to apply this all-important principle.

When we were ready to make hay, we first had to mow the field and then let the hay dry before we could take it into the barn (so it wouldn't combust and set the barn on fire). How long it takes for the hay to dry depends on the weather, the humidity, and the amount of sunshine. We had to pay close attention to the long-range weather predictions.

For years, we loaded all the hay on a wagon with a pitch

fork, but then my father got a piece of equipment called a "hay loader," which is pictured on the following page. It took four horses to pull it, because they were pulling both the wagon and the hay loader. The hay loader automatically picked up the hay and dropped it into the back of the wagon. We would have someone in the wagon with a fork, pitching the hay to another person up front.

On one occasion, there was an older gentleman helping in the front of the wagon, and I was in the back. The horses were continuing to pull the wagon, and it was moving while we worked. The hay loader deposited the hay in the back of the wagon, and it was my job to throw hay up to the older man and also to spread hay in my area, so I was doing two jobs and he was doing only one. Instead of spreading the hay evenly in his area, the older man was just spreading it around himself, getting deeper and deeper into a hole. Suddenly he realized that he couldn't get out from the hay piled around him and shouted, "Help!" I had to go help him, which I thought was very funny.

Part of keeping horses on the farm was taking them to the blacksmith shop regularly to be shoed. I remember Daddy saying to me, "Take this horse up to Mapleville." So I was off to the blacksmith shop, which was a fascinating place. There was always a fire going, as the blacksmith heated, hammered, and shaped the steel to make horseshoes and other metal items.

We had six horses. Some jobs, like plowing the garden or

The wagon and hay loader hitched to 4 horses

truck patch, plowing up potatoes, etc., required only one horse. In that case, we always used the lead horse (because he was the best at following instructions), so that horse really got a workout. To plow, we used two or three horses, depending on the type of plow, and other jobs, like pulling the wagon and hay loader, required up to four horses.

Anytime we needed to move something heavy on the farm, we moved it with horses. The picture of the hay loader on page 59 also shows how the horses looked after they were harnessed. First we would put on a horse collar, which went the whole way around the horse's neck and clamped shut to make it stationary. Then we took two wooden pieces called "the hanes" that fit around the collar into a groove, so the horse could pull a load. The harness had straps that went back the full length of the horse, with a leather strap that went across his rump and under his tail to hold it in place.

The wagon had a wooden tongue that extended out between the two back horses so that all of the horses would be pulling. Then, there were little chains called "traces." There was one of these on each side of the horse that went back and hooked to the wagon. The horses pulled the weight of the wagon by these chains.

Next we put on the headgear, which was called "the bridle." The lead horse is the one on the left in the front. There was a "jockey stick" that went from the collar of the lead horse to the bridle of the other front horse to keep them together. And there was a strap from the driver of the wagon to the lead horse called a "plow line." When the driver wanted to go right, he would jerk that line. If he wanted to go left, he would pull on the line. We also used verbal commands: "gee" to go right and "haw" to go left.

We spent a lot of time harnessing, unharnessing, feeding, watering, and bedding those horses. They were vitally important to our farming operation. This is such a big contrast to going out and jumping on a tractor today.

Our farm had one of the nicest wagon sheds I have ever seen. Most wagon sheds don't have two stories, but ours did. It also had three corn cribs, which is also unusual. The reason this building was called a wagon shed was because it was where we stored the big wagon bed.

The only time we used that large wagon bed was when we went up into the mountains to cut wood, which was a ten-mile round-trip, five miles up the mountain and five miles back. The people who owned the farm, the Doubs, also owned some mountain land, and that was where we went to cut wood. We did this in the fall after all the farm work was done for the year and after the leaves were off the trees. We needed to get a lot of wood to fuel the wood stove, heat our water to wash clothes and to use when we did butchering. We would usually go for wood on a Saturday, when we didn't have school. The large wagon we used to haul the wood was pulled by four horses.

First we looked for trees that weren't too large. If they

were too big, it meant a lot of extra work. In that case, we had to use heavy chisels, about an inch and a half thick and five or six inches long, and a sledge hammer to split the logs. To cut a tree in those days, we used an ax to take a big chip out of the side of the tree on the side where we wanted it to fall. Next we used a saw, which was six feet long and had a handle on each end. With one man on each end of the saw, we would saw into the back of the tree where we had taken the chip out.

This was very hard work. We kept on sawing back and forth until the tree fell, and then we sawed it into sections about eight feet long. If they were longer than that, they were too difficult for us to lift onto the wagon.

We worked all day, stopping only for lunch, which was usually a cold pudding sandwich. When we had enough wood for a load, we would start down the mountain.

The wagon we used for this work was the only piece of equipment on the farm that had brakes. With anything else, the horses could hold back on it with their collars, but this wagon was too heavy, and we had to go down a very steep hill. There was a bar on the wagon about five feet long, and when we pulled it, the brakes would be applied.

The brakes themselves consisted of nothing more than blocks of wood in front of the two back wheels. When we pulled on the bar, it would push those blocks of wood against the wheel. When we got ready to go down the steep hill, we put the brakes on, and the wheels wouldn't go around at all. So we slid the whole way down. If a safety inspector were to see young boys doing such a thing today, it would make him crazy. But that was a different time. Our father allowed us to do that extremely dangerous work.

When we got home with the wood, we had to unload it. Then a man came with a tractor. We connected our saw to the tractor with a belt and let the tractor sit running. This provided power for the saw, which we then used to cut the wood into manageable pieces.

The saw was about a foot and half round, and had an attached table. We lifted each of the eight-foot-long pieces of wood up onto that table and pushed them through the saw to make pieces short enough to be used in the wood stove. As the logs were cut into more manageable lengths, the resulting pieces were thrown onto a pile, to be split later with an ax. We discovered that wood would split better after it had been through a frost. Once split, the wood was carried in to supply the wood box on the back porch.

Cutting wood was one job I really did not enjoy, so I made myself a pledge that I would never have a wood stove, and to this day I have kept that vow. The first house I bought had a wood stove in it, but it didn't take me long to get rid of it.

The busiest day of the year, for us, was butchering day. That day we butchered four hogs. This took all day, even though friends and neighbors came to help. We started early in the morning and wouldn't get done until after dark, and we were on our feet moving all that time.

First we had to shoot and kill the hogs and bleed them out. Once, when I was at my grandparents' on butchering day, they shot a hog and stuck it, but it kept moving around, so they had to shoot it again. That was the only time it ever happened in all the butchering I attended.

Next, we had to scald the hog to get the hair off. We used a thermometer to make sure the water was hot enough before putting it in a trough. Then we tied a rope around the body of the hog, and four or five men would pick up the hog (which weighed four or five hundred pounds), and put it into that scalding-hot water. We used the rope to move the hog around in the water, making sure all the parts of its body were covered.

After scalding the hog, we would put it on a scaffold, and three or four men would use scrapers (made of wood with metal blades on each end), to scrape all the hair off the hog. These scrapers were about six inches long and had a large, round, metal blade about five inches across on one end and a smaller blade, about three inches across, on the other end. It took quite a while to get all the hair off of a hog, even with several of us working on it at once.

After the hair was all off, we would hang the hog on a tripod-shaped wooden frame. This was eight or nine feet tall and would hold the hog up off of the ground. There were hooks in this apparatus, and we cut a slit in the hog's leg and hung it up so that we could clean and gut it and then cut it apart.

When we butchered, we had two kettles side by side that we used to cook the pudding, *pon haus*[4] and lard. The rinds, parts of the head, the liver, and the heart were cooked up to make pudding. This had to be stirred constantly with a stirrer that had a long wooden handle and a metal hook at the end (which we used to scratch the bottom of the kettle to keep the meat from sticking). This cooking and stirring took about an hour. The *pon haus* was made by adding cornmeal to the broth off the pudding. This also had to be cooked and stirred. We often had the pudding for breakfast, cooked with hominy and onions. The *pon haus* could be sliced, fried crisp, and served with syrup.

Any fat we removed from the hog was made into lard. We cut the fat lengthwise and crosswise until we had small pieces, then cooked them in a kettle and used a dipper with holes in it to strain out any large pieces. Next we would strain the liquid lard through cheesecloth and into lard cans, which held approximately four gallons each. This lard was used for all our cooking and baking.

To make cracklings, we would take the pieces of lard we had dipped out and the pieces that were left in the cheesecloth after straining and put them in the sausage stuffer and crank it to squeeze all the juice out. What was left after the

---

4   Otherwise known as scrapple, this farm delight is a mush of pork broth combined with cornmeal. This is put into loaf-shaped pans and then sliced and fried. It is usually served with molasses for breakfast.

juice was out was called "cracklings," and was formed into cakes. We would break this apart and use it, along with potatoes and sausage, in the stuffing for the hog maw, made from the stomach of the hog.[5] We also made souse out of the snout, feet, and head.

The women cleaned the casings, the intestines of the hog, and they were used for making sausage. The casings were then stuffed, using a sausage stuffer.

We cut the hog into hams, shoulders, sides, spareribs, tenderloin, and backbones. Then we took the hams, shoulders, and sides into the basement, where we had a table to lay them on, and we sugar-cured them with a special mixture containing brown sugar, salt, and salt peter. We put this mixture in a washtub, put the meat in, and rubbed the mixture onto the meat, using our fingers to get the sugar-cure up under the skin at the ends of the legs. This sugar-cured meat was kept in the basement for two or three weeks and was then taken to the smokehouse.

The smokehouse had one door but no windows. The meat was hung from the beams of the smokehouse, and then we had to produce smoke. To produce it, we used a bucket and put into it some green wood that wouldn't burn; it would just sit there and smoke. We let the meat smoke for two or

5   *Hog maw* is a Pennsylvania Dutch dish made from a cleaned pig's stomach, traditionally stuffed with cubed potatoes and loose pork sausage. Other ingredients include cabbage, onions, and spices. It was traditionally boiled in a large pot covered in water, but it can also be baked or broiled until browned or split. Then it is drizzled with butter before being served.

three days. The hams and other cured meats were stored in the smokehouse, and they needed no refrigeration because the sugar-curing and smoking preserved them.

Even though butchering was very hard work, no one got paid for doing it. Instead, we would give each person who helped a "mess" of sausage, *pon haus,* or pudding. When our neighbors were ready to butcher, we went to their farms and helped them. Other people came to the farm on butchering day, wanting to buy some of the meat. This would not be allowed today, and farmers can no longer do their own butchering, unless they have qualified and licensed inspectors present. How times have changed!

CHAPTER THREE

LIFE IN THE NAVY

I graduated from high school in June of 1946 with no solid idea of what I wanted to do with my life. My brother Seibert had just gotten out of the Navy, so I thought, "Why not try that?" I had no permanent girl friend at the time and nothing else to hold me back, so on June 25, 1946, I joined the Navy for two years and was sent to Bainbridge, Maryland, for boot camp.

As our bus pulled into the camp, the older sailors kept shouting to us, "You'll be sorry!" What a greeting! It certainly didn't do much to calm our nerves or lift our spirits. This was a brand-new experience, and most of us were away from home for the first time. We didn't know what to think. It sure wasn't the kind of reception I was expecting.

A lot of Navy men joined up with a buddy or classmate, but when I went in, I didn't know anyone. I was all alone, and it was a rather scary feeling to venture out into the world without family or friends. But I soon had a lot of new friends.

I was surprised that some of the men joining the Navy didn't know how to swim, and I was glad that my brothers and I had learned back at Beaver Creek near our farm.

You Can't Outgive God

I was placed in a barracks with many other young men who were also new to the Navy. Every day we would march to and from class singing songs. We spent quite a bit of time on guard duty, watching the clothesline or the garbage pile for four hours at a time, sometimes in the pouring rain. My observation about the Navy was that they were always in a hurry to have us do everything, and then we ended up sitting around a lot, waiting on our next order. If any of us talked too much while standing in line, that person had to put his hat in his mouth.

When we got paid, one officer would give out the money we had earned, but then, as we moved on down the line, others would be there to take out money for this or that. During my time in the Navy, I managed to save nearly enough to pay for a brand-new 1948 Studebaker when I got back home.

One guy in our outfit was always so hard-up for cash that if you would lend him $5 until payday, he would then give you back $10. That was an attractive deal to me, and I did it many times.

When we first got to boot camp, we weren't allowed to go anywhere, so we were stuck in the housing area. After a few weeks, they finally allowed us to go to the PX. I was so glad to get some freedom that I ate a quart and a half of ice cream. I enjoyed the ice cream. But going to the PX was not entirely a good experience. While I was there, I saw a nearby field of corn, and that reminded me of Boonsboro and home and made me very homesick.

I remember receiving letters from some of my old girl-friends. One of them, when I didn't answer her, wrote me another letter. It contained just these few words: "I'm still living."

Ruth Baker, another of my old girlfriends, surprised me by coming with my parents to visit me twice while I was in boot camp. We had dated quite a bit in high school. I would go over to her house on my bicycle, since our family had only one car and several drivers. After a while, however, I felt that Ruth and I were getting too serious for as young as we were, and I broke off the relationship and dated a lot of other girls. Apparently Ruth hadn't given up on me. Aside from those two visits (and another one after I had gradu-ated from boot camp), she wrote me many letters while I was in the Navy.

After boot camp, I left Bainbridge and spent a twelve-day leave at home with my family. A few of my Navy friends, Sponseller and Shindle (from Hagerstown) and Talbert (from Ashville, North Carolina), came to our farm and spent the night, all of us returning to Bainbridge on September 10. Then, on September 20, 1946, we were sent to Quonset, Rhode Island, where we were assigned to an aircraft carrier, The U.S.S. Philippine Sea.

My quarters were in a compartment between the hangar and flight decks. About a hundred of us shared a very small living area there. It was extremely tight quarters, and our bunks were three high. I had the middle bunk. I happened to be next to the head boatsman, who was an old timer, and he looked out for me.

On an aircraft carrier, the flight deck is where the planes land and take off, and the hangar deck is where the planes are stored. Out of a crew of about a dozen men, I was asked to be in charge of operating one of the three elevators that took the planes up and down between those decks. It was a very important job, because about a hundred planes would take off and land in a little over half an hour. It was very exciting being on that ship.

During the time I was on The U.S.S. Philippine Sea, I went on three different shakedown cruises, the first in the fall of 1946, before we went to the South Pole. When a new crew comes onto a ship, they take a shakedown cruise, and every type of operation and maneuver imaginable is executed. This included making a continuous circuit of landings and takeoffs, gunnery practice in conjunction with aircraft, night operations, fueling at sea, and daily general quarters. The successful completion of such a shakedown cruise leaves a crew well trained in their duties, general seamanship, and emergency procedures.

During each shakedown cruise, the ship operated off of Cuba, occasionally dropping anchor at Guantanamo Bay. We would dock out in the bay and take a small boat ashore. I went there three different times.

Guantanamo Bay wasn't very important at the time. That was long before anyone had ever thought of housing

In my Navy days

prisoners of war there. We loved to go to shore simply because there was a PX there, with food items that we could purchase.

I was one of a very fortunate group of young sailors who got to participate in something very special called "Operation Highjump." This was the Navy's Antarctic expedition of 1946–47. Ten different ships took part in the expedition, and The U.S.S. Philippine Sea, on which I was assigned, was one of those ships.

On December 24, 1946, I was given a leave to spend Christmas at home with my family, and had another 72-hour leave on December 30. After that leave, my parents took me to Norfolk, Virginia, where I was to board the ship for the trip to the South Pole. Ruth came along to see me off, and the four of us traveled all the way to Norfolk in the snow and rain. On January 1, 1947, my parents and Ruth went to the harbor and were permitted to board my ship, which my mother later described as a trip she would never forget.

On January 2, 1947, I said goodbye to my parents and Ruth, and we sailed from Norfolk at noon with Rear Admiral Richard E. Byrd on board. He was accompanied by his staff, six R4D transports and more than a hundred tons of cargo, including two complete airplanes in crates. From Norfolk, the carrier headed for the Panama Canal. Our ship was the largest to go through the canal up to that time. It was so wide that our gun turrets hit the side of the canal, causing some minor damage to the ship. Little cars called "donkeys" were used to pull the ships through the canal. When I heard about them, being the farm boy I was, I was expecting to see real donkeys.

On January 10, 1947, we began what, at that time, was the longest non-stop voyage ever made by any ship. A great fanfare was made when we crossed the Equator or what the Navy men called "crossing the line." The guys who had crossed the Equator before did a type of initiation on us who were new to the experience, making some of the fellows dress up like girls, and giving us a hard time — all in the name of good, clean fun. This was a memorable occasion, which lasted two days. A copy of the certificate I received for crossing the Equator is on the following page.

Even more valued, because of its rarity, was the membership awarded the crew in the "Royal Order of the Penguin," for going to the South Pole with Admiral Byrd. That certificate was signed by the Admiral himself. It is pictured on page 77.

Our crew was not permitted to leave the ship at the South Pole. We had been issued equipment to withstand temperatures to 90 degrees below zero, but it wasn't all that cold there. It didn't seem so different from our winters back home.

During the trip, Admiral Byrd would walk up and down the flight deck to get exercise. Since my job was to operate the elevator that brought the planes up to the flight deck, I often saw him taking his walk and was able to get his personal autograph. I cherished that and carried it in my wallet for many years.

The certificate Jim received for crossing the Equator

The certificate Jim received for traveling to the South Pole, signed by Rear Admiral Richard E. Byrd

On January 23, 1947, we sighted the first iceberg of hundreds we would encounter. The six R4D's, with Admiral Byrd in the first, flew off the ship on the 29th and 30th of January, 1947. These planes took off from our flight deck on wheels, but when they landed, they were on skis. The planes all arrived safely in Little America. They were the largest planes ever to take off from the deck of any carrier, and they were purposely left at the South Pole, buried in the snow.

While there, it was our job to transfer the hundred tons of supplies from The U.S.S. Philippine Sea to another ship. We accomplished that.

Then, on February 6, 1947, we started the long voyage back home. It was amazing how much rough water we passed through. On February 11th, my sister Elfleta was listening to the radio and heard that our expedition was in a terrible blizzard, with wind speeds of up to 50 MPH and huge cakes of ice. It was a very rough storm, and while it raged, our ship was near a standstill. But, thank God, we made it safely home.

That aircraft carrier was about a thousand feet long, and I could stand at one end of it and watch it bow in the middle. I always marveled at that fact, thinking that something so huge might break in two.

My mother kept an extensive scrapbook of all the newspaper articles that were written about our expedition. Apparently those articles had kept the folks back home well informed about the trip and its purpose. When I got back to Panama, they gave us all the mail that had been sent to us while we were gone. There were about sixty letters for me from friends and family. Sixteen of those letters were from Ruth, the girl who was later to become my wife.

When we got into Panama, Mardi Gras was in full swing, and we were allowed our first leave after spending so much time on the ship. As always, with Mardi Gras, there was a lot of excitement and a real party atmosphere. The main thing I remember is that a lot of my buddies went out to enjoy themselves and came back very drunk. The U.S.S. Philippine Sea arrived back at Quonset on February 27, 1947, after an 18,000-mile round trip that took thirty-nine days, which was, at that time, the longest non-stop voyage made by any ship.

While at Quonset, our off hours were spent on the basket-ball court, which brought back many good memories from high school. We also had a unique way of showing movies on the ship, by putting the movie screen on one of the big elevators and raising it just enough so that everyone could gather round and see the film.

In April of 1947, The U.S.S. Philippine Sea did another shakedown cruise, in which I participated. During this cruise, we were allowed to sign up to go on one of the flights that took off from the ship. I signed up, but the more I thought about it the less I wanted to try this new experience for myself. If you wanted to go, you had to sign your life insurance away. I kept thinking, "Suppose I get some happy-go-lucky pilot; it's hard to tell what might happen!" So, in the end, I lost my nerve and cancelled.

During this particular shakedown cruise, we went to Cuba, and they let us go on leave in the country. I was one of those chosen to take a train from Guantanamo Bay into Havana. This was probably because I always followed orders and tried to do my best at whatever I was asked to do. There were about three thousand men on the ship, and they only let a small number of us go. It wasn't much of a sightseeing tour. I was surprised to see how poor the people were and appalled by their living conditions.

At the completion of this shakedown cruise, our ship was put in dry dock in the Brooklyn Navy Yard in New York, for repairs. We were there about six weeks. It was very interesting to see our ship in dry dock. Now I could see how large the bottom of the ship was. There was as much under the water as above.

While the ship was in dry dock, I took the subway heading toward home and went all the way to the Holland Tunnel. It cost me a nickel. Then I started thumbing a ride, and a guy who was also in the Navy picked me up, bought me a meal, and took me all the way to Baltimore. From there, I was able to thumb it the rest of the way home. So that nickel was all that I spent to get home to Maryland from New York.

During that time, I must have come home about every other week, many times by hitchhiking a ride, the same method of transportation I had used when I was late going home from high school. I wouldn't recommend doing that these days, because it wouldn't be safe, but in those days it was a common practice and not considered dangerous at all.

Another time, when I was thumbing a ride, a lady picked me up. In the middle of the night, I fell asleep and didn't wake up until we were in Philadelphia. She had apparently gotten lost. She took me to the bus station, and I had to get a bus home. Trucks would often pick me up, but when we got to the ferry at Wilmington, Delaware, they would always make me get out, so they wouldn't get in trouble. Later they would meet me on the ferry and let me get back in.

Woody came to New York to see me, and we went to some shows together. One of the other guys from my ship was from New York, and he wanted to take me home to meet and date his sister.

When our ship got out of dry dock, I went on my third and final shakedown cruise. The ship was going to Europe next, and it wouldn't be back in time for my discharge from the Navy. I had enlisted for two years and was due to get out in June of 1948. So the Navy sent me back to Quonset, Rhode Island, and I was put to work there, punching a cash register in the commissary. After living on the farm, where we had raised and grown all our own food, I was amazed to see how big some of the men's grocery bills were. They were being paid once every two weeks, so they were buying enough groceries to last them until their next pay.

While I was there, I also worked as a waiter in the officers' club. This was easy work for me, after the farm and my time at sea. Sometimes I was given tips just for doing my job. I wasn't accustomed to making money that easily. Doing strenuous farm work, I had worked all day for just a few dollars.

While stationed at Quonset, I had the opportunity to visit the son of the Doub Family who owned the farm our family was renting. He was living in Boston, Massachusetts, and I took a bus there and back.

I served twenty-two months in the Navy, receiving my discharge in April, 1948. I made some wonderful friends while in the Navy. One guy from Ashville, North Carolina, remained my friend until he died. He became a real estate agent, and when I went down to Ashville to visit him, he would meet me dressed as if he was very poor. As we drove down the streets, he would point at buildings and houses and say, "I own that. I own that. Etc." It just goes to show that you can't judge a book by its cover.

I visited another Navy buddy after Ruth and I were married and had our two sons. This guy's father owned an ice cream business. While we were there, I could have all the ice cream I wanted. My buddy also owned a cabin on a lake, and first thing each morning he would go out and jump into the cold water — even colder than the water in Beaver Creek back home.

I consider it a great blessing to have served in the U.S. Navy and also that I joined up when I did. It was the only time I know of when you could enlist for a period of just two years. The usual enlistment they required was a period of three or four years, and if you desired you could even enlist for up to six years. Joining the Navy when I did also kept me from having to serve in the Korean War. The only injury I sustained in my time of service to our country came when a can of ammunition dropped on my finger, smashing it. That finger is still flat to this day, but that injury was very minor compared to the injuries and loss of life sustained by many of those who served in the Korean War.

It was exciting to have the opportunity to go through the Panama Canal, to cross the Equator, and to travel to the South Pole with Admiral Byrd. I had the opportunity to travel over 20,000 miles – 18,000 to the South Pole and back and the rest when our ship traveled to Cuba three times. I enjoyed seeing the many beautiful colors of the ocean water and the icebergs at the South Pole.

The six weeks I spent in New York while our ship was in dry dock was also a special time. All of these are experiences that I will never forget. There are also some practical benefits that are mine because I was in the Navy. As I have grown older, I have begun to require more medications, and I am able to get them through the Veterans Administration.

The most memorable moment of my Navy career was coming into New York Harbor after traveling to the South Pole and back. There stood our beautiful Statue of Liberty with the burning torch. I remember getting goose bumps when I saw it. I stood there gazing at her and thinking of the richness of our nation and how proud I was to have served. To this day, I experience that pride each time I am able to stand up on Memorial Day or any other time veterans are honored. It gives me a deep sense of satisfaction to know that I had the privilege of serving my country in this way.

CHAPTER FOUR

GOD'S FINGERPRINTS

As I look back on my life, I see many things that I really believe were arranged by God on my behalf. For example, a very interesting thing happened with regard to the end of my Naval service. The Navy could have easily kept me working in the commissary and the officers' club in Rhode Island until my release date, which was to be in June of 1948, but, instead they decided to release me two months early. Rather than wait until June, they discharged me in April. There was no special reason they didn't release me sooner or that they didn't keep me until my scheduled release date, but I know now that this, as with so many other things, was God's perfect timing.

For my part, I was ready to get back to Boonsboro and enjoy some time with my family — and with Ruth Baker. I went back to live on the farm with my parents for about a year, and, during that time, I attended Ruth's high school graduation and escorted her to her Senior Prom. It was easier for me to get around now, because I had purchased a brand-new 1948 Studebaker, (which cost me about $2,800).

I still wasn't sure of what kind of work I wanted to do. At first, I thought of going to college under the GI Bill to prepare to teach Physical Education. After all, because I was a veteran, Uncle Sam would have picked up the tab for me. But the more I thought about it, the more I knew I just couldn't do it. I didn't want to become a student again and sit for months or years in a classroom.

I next began to consider becoming a salesman, since I liked working with people, but I never got the chance to look for work in that field. God had something else in mind.

My brother Seibert had become an electrician while he was in the Navy, and this led to his finding a job with Potomac Edison, the power company, in nearby Hagerstown, Maryland, as a meter tester. Now he learned that the company needed another man on their crew. The work would be reading meters and doing service work in the Boonsboro area, and when he told me about the job, I went and applied for it immediately.

The Boonsboro branch of Potomac Edison was housed in a small building on Main Street. It was just a big room, with no partitions, and that one room contained both a store and an office. There was one large desk in the office area. The manager sat on one side of it, and the secretary sat on the other side. This was the only furniture in the place, other than a few chairs where visitors could sit. The other part of the room was the appliance store. There was an upstairs, where they kept parts we used to repair appliances and a small bathroom.

Seibert was a very good worker, and so I suppose the manager of PE thought I would be, too. After the interview, he told me he had liked everything he heard, but he would have to speak with his boss in Hagerstown and see if he was in agreement with hiring me.

He called me later and said that I had the job and would start on May 19, 1948. Without my early discharge from the Navy, I would have still been in Rhode Island at that time. There were a lot of guys getting out of the service and needing jobs, and, if I hadn't received that early discharge, someone else would surely have gotten that job.

Working for the power company and my close connections with the people on my meter route proved to be a very important part of God's plans for my future. I ended up working for Potomac Edison for the next twelve years.

As soon as I got the job with PE, they provided me a pickup truck to drive. That was great. On the farm, I had rarely gotten to drive, since we had only one vehicle and four drivers. I hadn't even gotten my driver's license until I was 17. And while I was in the Navy for those two years, I couldn't drive. We had no cars or trucks on the ship. Now I was driving thousands of miles a year.

The truck was very light and had no weight in the rear, so it didn't do well in snow or ice, and I had to be very careful with it in inclement weather. Once, when I was driving, the truck hit a patch of ice. I had been going south, but suddenly I did a 180 and ended up facing north. But, in general, life was good, and I was blessed.

I was thankful to Seibert for helping me land the job. He got married that July, to a girl named Mary, whom he had met at the Braddock Heights Roller Skating Rink. After they were married, they lived for a while in the four-room apartment in the stone house on our farm.

I was blessed with three brothers and a sister, and we were always there for each other. I realize that this is not true in every family. All of us would do well finding jobs and would be able to buy our own homes. We would all get married and stay married and have children. When any of us had a problem, the others were there to help.

I've heard it said that you should never deal with your family in business, but I have not found this to be true with my own family. They have given me great support, and I've always tried to help them, including my nieces and nephews. Over the years, we have spent time together doing things like playing ball, and they are all still great friends with me today.

Things were going well for me on another front. Even though my parents were Christians, and I had gone to church all my life, my memories of our older minister were that his prayers were about as long as his sermons. When I came back home now, the church had a younger minister, a middle-aged man, and the two of us got along very well. He had the kind of personality that could relate to anyone, young, old or in-between. His name was Curvin Thompson, and Ruth and I both liked him a lot. He was a great fisherman and storyteller and became one of my best friends.

Our church was small, but we had a rather large youth group composed of about a dozen kids. One time a ministerial student came to speak to us about friendship. I remember him telling us that if a person has two or three really good friends that he can rely on in times of trouble, he has done well. He said that a few friends you can trust and share your heart with are probably all you will have in your lifetime, and you should count yourself blessed to have them. I have had some wonderful friends, and, as you read this book, you will see the great people who have helped me along the way. Early on, I learned that if you want friends you must be a friend.

We also had a marvelous Sunday school teacher. He had the gift of being able to teach without reading or using a lot of notes. He was such an interesting speaker that we had twenty to twenty-five men attending Sunday School every Sunday morning, which has never happened before or since. This was nearly unheard of, since many men don't like to attend Sunday School. One of the men in our class ran Kline's Mill and was active in the community, serving as president of Washington County Hospital.

Our teacher told us stories of people who were giving ninety percent of their income and how God was blessing them. One day he told us about a group of men who would sit around in the Mapleville store and talk. There was a family in the area that had experienced a fire, and all the men were saying how sorry they felt that this had happened to them. Then, one man, who was a school teacher, stood up and said, "I feel sorry for them, so I'm going to give them

$10!" This, he showed us, was a more appropriate response to their tragedy. This teacher had a way of driving his point home.

One member of the class, who always had a lot to say, told us one Sunday, "Those guys took my son out and got him drunk."

The teacher's wise reply to this was: "No, your son went out and got himself drunk." What a wise man he was!

This teacher and I became good friends, and I worked for him on Saturdays on his farm.

The same year I got out of the Navy I was going home one night from a date with Ruth. They were redoing the road in an area of Route 40-A, right across from the big stone house that Ruth and I would later purchase, and the workers had left a huge steamroller sitting by the side of the road. A car with three men in it had come from Middletown, and as they came down the hill, they crossed the road and hit that steamroller, killing all of them instantly. As the first person on the scene of the accident, I found them all three sitting in the car, just as if they had been asleep. They were apparently going too fast and lost control of the car, and the force of the crash must have broken their necks.

This tragedy left a lasting impression on me. It reminded me of how fragile life is and how quickly, without warning, it can be lost. I feel sure that it never occurred to those men when they left home that they might not be returning. Every one of us will face eternity at some future moment. The important question we must each ask ourselves is, "Will I be ready?"

CHAPTER FIVE

MARRYING RUTH BAKER

I need to tell you more about Ruth Baker, the girl who was to become my bride. Ruth was two years younger than I, and we went to Sunday school together. Like my father, her dad was a very good farmer and bought a 170-acre farm with a stone house, big bank barn, and some other buildings, including a spring house, where they got their water. The Baker farm had a nice meadow and a creek where we went swimming. That creek is now a trout stream that is stocked with trout every year, but there were no trout in it back then. But it was so nice that people would come there and bring a blanket to spread out on the ground along the creek and have a picnic. Our farm was level, but this one had rolling hills.

Ruth's father had been doing so well that he had bought a brand-new 1937 Plymouth. Then, the very next year, when he was only 44 years old, he was diagnosed with liver cancer. He never left the hospital, but died just ten days after his diagnosis. I remember that my parents took me to my grandfather's house the day of the funeral, and I stayed with him while my grandmother and my parents went to Mr. Baker's funeral.

You Can't Outgive God

Ruth's dad was a fine man, and those who knew him were very sad when he died. He and Mrs. Baker had four children. The oldest, Luther, was twenty years old when their father died. The eldest daughter, Frances, was eighteen, Becky was fourteen, and Ruth was just eleven. Ruth had always been an excellent student, but she was so upset over her father's death that she failed to pass to the next grade that year. She was a very caring person, and her father's death was extremely difficult for her.

During the elementary grades, Ruth and Becky went to a 2-room school at Lappans Crossroads. Ruth liked music, and that school had a special music class an hour each week. Ruth signed up for the music class, and that was probably where she learned to play the mandolin and sing. Later Becky and Ruth both went to Boonsboro High School, where Ruth took the academic course and made good grades.

When Ruth and I began to like each other, we couldn't really go anywhere because I didn't have a car. As I noted earlier, I went to visit her on my bicycle. We dated for a good while, but then we started to get too serious, and, because we were so young, I broke it off. When I went in the Navy, I had been dating other girls, but I wasn't interested in anyone in particular. Ruth's mother and my mother went to the same church and were in the same Sunday school class. I guess her mother told my mother that Ruth would like to go along to visit me. I was only too happy to see her, and that's how we got back together.

After their father died, Luther married, lived in the stone house on the farm, and ran the farm for about ten years. During that time, Frances left home, got married and had three children of her own. Mrs. Baker, who never remarried, decided to build a little bungalow about a quarter of a mile up the road, with two bedrooms, a kitchen, a living room, and a small bathroom. It also had a front porch and another porch at the end of the house, and a nice yard and vegetable garden. She and the girls lived there.

When they needed milk, Ruth would just walk up to the barn and milk one of the cows. Other than the small amount of milk they used, the rest of the milk supply was skimmed off and used to make butter.

Around 1950, Luther decided not to farm anymore, and so the Baker farm was sold. By that time, Ruth and I were married. Before I tell you about that, let me tell you about a man God brought into our lives, who made a great impact on us all. His name was Mr. Harry Newcomer, and he was the Register of Wills for Washington County. He was also a member of our church, Superintendant of our Sunday school, President of the Church Council, and church Treasurer. When he was ready to retire from his position as Treasurer of the church, he asked me to take that job. I had been treasurer for a building project earlier and learned that it wasn't something I enjoyed, so I declined the offer. Mr. Newcomer was disappointed. He often reminded me that we were distantly related, going back to my great-great-grandfather's era, when he had owned the Benevola store.

Aside from all of his other roles, every Sunday morning Mr. Newcomer would stand near the door of the church and greet people as they came into the sanctuary. He hadn't been appointed to do this, but he just had a love for the Lord and for people. He was always trying to get the young people of the church involved in something so they would become leaders. I cherished his friendship.

Ruth graduated from Boonsboro High School in 1948, just after I got out of the Navy. Mr. Newcomer really liked her, and so he now asked her to be his secretary in the Register of Wills office. She didn't have a business education, but when he offered her the job, he said she could take off in the afternoons and go to the community college to learn shorthand and typing and the other skills she would need to do the job well. Ruth had wanted to work for a while before we got married, so she agreed to work for Mr. Newcomer, and worked there for about a year and a half. During that time, she drove back and forth to work in the 1937 Plymouth that had been her father's.

I was working for the power company forty hours a week and still living on the farm with my parents and my younger brother Charles. Woody had a steady girlfriend and Ruth's sister, Becky, had a boyfriend.

Ruth and I were in the same Sunday school class and Youth Fellowship. She and I usually went out on dates a couple of times a week, often double-dating with Becky and her boyfriend, who had a car with a rumble seat. For those who don't remember, a rumble seat was sort of like a trunk that opened from the top and had seats inside. Ruth and I rode in that rumble seat, and we would all go to the movies in Boonsboro (which cost 15 cents at that time).

Before the main feature, the theater would show something called a "serial." This was a series that left you hanging and kept you coming back to find out what would happen next. Even if we didn't particularly like or want to see the next main feature, we had to keep going back to see the next part of the serial.

Ruth's brother Luther and I became good friends. Because he was a farmer, and I knew a lot about farming, we got along well. He liked to kid me. Because I didn't have enough whiskers to make it necessary for me to shave yet, he told me I wasn't a man. I don't remember exactly when I did start to shave, but it was a good while after that. Even today, I would never have enough whiskers to grow a decent beard.

Ruth and I decided we would get married on November 23, 1949, the day before Thanksgiving. I had a week's paid vacation coming from the power company, and I also had Thanksgiving Day off, so if I took off the day after Thanksgiving, which was a Friday, we would have eleven days for a honeymoon. I wanted to give Ruth a very nice honeymoon.

You Can't Outgive God

Since she had never traveled, I decided to take Ruth to Florida. But, for that, I would need more money. Then the thought came to me, "Why not make some extra money husking corn to help pay for the honeymoon?" My father knew I was a good corn husker, and he said he would give me 30 cents a shock to husk corn.

I worked very hard to earn the money for our honeymoon. I started out early each morning, before it was daylight and husked corn as long as I could before reporting for work at the power company at 8 A.M. The best time to throw shocks of corn down and husk them is in the morning, when there is dew on the ground. I threw a lot of shocks down, and

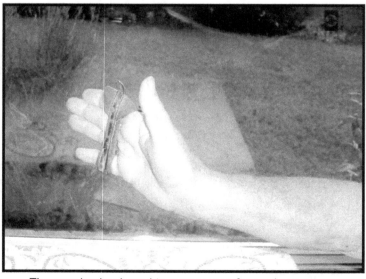

The corn husker I used to earn money for our honeymoon
The husker and the corn chopper together
would have cost less than $10.

the bottoms of them would stay moist, so they weren't as hard on my hands. You can't wear gloves to husk corn, so my hands got pretty tough.

Many evenings, when I got home from work, I went out and husked more corn. I also husked corn all day every Saturday. To do this, I got down on my knees and used a corn husker, which is pictured on the previous page. Altogether I husked about 70,000 ears of corn, or 500 shocks, each of which would contain about 140 ears. This was about 25 acres of corn. So you can get an idea of how much work this was, a 25-acre field is pictured on page 99. I was paid 30 cents a shock, so I made $150, which was almost enough to pay for the honeymoon.

As time neared for our wedding, I asked our pastor, Curvin Thompson, how much he would charge to perform the ceremony. Always jovial, his answer was that he didn't take money from just everyone. He would take it from some, but not from others. I got an idea: I found a cigar box and put $10 worth of pennies (which was more than a day's wages) and a brick inside and presented it to him. He had a good laugh over this, and from time to time he referred to it and said I had short-changed him. We did a lot of joking back and forth about it. He continued to talk about that until the day he died. Years later, when we celebrated my 80th birthday, he had already passed away, but his wife came to the party and brought me a very special gift — a cigar box with $10 worth of pennies inside.

You Can't Outgive God

Ruth and I were married at the Benevola United Brethren Church at 7 o'clock in the evening on November 23, 1949. It was a large wedding for those days, attended by more than a hundred people. Our good friend, Rev. Curvin Thompson performed the ceremony, and Ruth's older brother, Luther, walked her down the aisle.

Ruth was a beautiful bride, dressed in a full- length white slipper satin gown with a full court train. Her sister, Becky, was her maid of honor, and my brother, Seibert, was my best man.

It was customary in those days, when someone got married, for his friends to do something to his car, sometimes tying tin cans to the back or putting soap on the windows. I knew Ruth's brother would have plans for my Studebaker, so I had someone follow me into Boonsboro, which is three miles from the church, and I parked my car in an alley where I didn't think Luther would find it. After the ceremony, we had a reception, which took a good while. Then Ruth changed into a pretty green suit, and I had someone take us into Boonsboro to get the car.

But guess what I found? My car had been jacked up and set up on concrete blocks, so I couldn't move it at all. Luther and his friends had their laugh and kept us from leaving for a little while, but they finally took my car down and let us get on our way. I was glad I had made reservations for us to spend the night in nearby Frederick, before leaving for Florida.

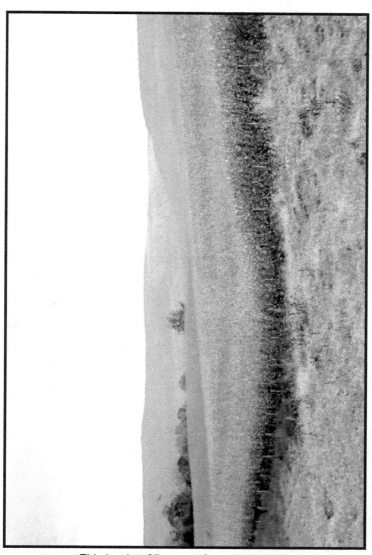

This is what 25 acres of corn looks like.

You Can't Outgive God

Roads in those days weren't very good, and it took us about three days to get to Miami, which was more than a thousand miles away. We stopped along the way to visit someone and also to see some of the sights. At one motel where we stopped, the lady said, "Oh, a honeymoon couple? I have a special room for you."

I said, "Let's see what's special about it." She took us in and showed us the room and said it was $5 a night. I said, "Don't you have anything less expensive?" She said she did and took us to another room. I said, "Well, I don't see any difference." She said the difference was the curtains. I wasn't about to pay that woman $5 for her "special room," and decided that I didn't even want to pay her $3 for the other room (because of the way she had tried to take advantage of us). Ruth and I got back in the car and went on down the road, where we stayed at another motel for $3. I had husked a lot of corn for that money, and I wasn't about to give it up so easily.

A funny thing happened while I was driving in Florida. I was following behind another car in traffic, and the driver pulled over and told me to go on around him. He said I was making him nervous. I hadn't been aware that I was doing anything to make him nervous.

Ruth really enjoyed our stay in Florida, especially eating in the local restaurants. There were lots of different foods she had never tasted before. She also enjoyed seeing the sights in Florida because it was all new to her, since she had never had the opportunity to travel.

Marrying Ruth Baker

After a wonderful honeymoon, it was time to head back to Boonsboro. In those days, when you returned from your honeymoon, your friends "banded" you. As many of them as possible would get together and shoot off a shotgun, beat on pots and pans, or anything else they could do to make noise. About 30 or 40 people showed up to band us. The men found a fence rail, put me on it, and carried me around.

After we were married, Ruth and I lived with her mother in the bungalow for the next couple of years. We never gave much thought to moving, because she wanted us to live with her.

Ruth continued working for Mr. Newcomer at the Register of Wills office. He was a great encouragement to both of us, and now we also became good workers in the church. Ruth had a lovely voice, and she sang solos for weddings and other special occasions. She loved music and was in charge of the junior choir. I can remember the good times we had with those young people, especially when we had parties for them at Christmastime. I served as Treasurer of the building committee, head of the trustees, and held many other offices and positions over the years.

Ruth enjoyed her job at the Register of Wills office and she was well-liked by the other people working there. She loved seeing and talking to those who came into the office, and she appreciated the fact that Mr. Newcomer had given her time off to attend school and prepare for the job. Other than Mr.

Newcomer, there were two older men working there. One of them was married, but the other one had never married. One afternoon Ruth thought it was quitting time, so she got her coat on and told everyone she would see them the next day. When she got home, she looked at the clock and realized that she had left work an hour early. She got a lot of kidding about that.

The Register of Wills office was near the street, and the place where they auctioned off houses was right in front of their office. One day Ruth came home and told me about a house that had been put up for sale in front of the court house and hadn't brought enough money. She said that Mr. Newcomer thought we should buy the house, so we went to look at it and ended up buying it for $7,200 and the taxes, which were $29 a year. That was in 1951, and Ruth and I were both working. I had started out making 80 cents an hour, when I went to work in 1948, and, by the time we bought the house, I was making around $1.00 an hour. Since we were both working and had no children yet, we could afford the house.

We had managed to save a good bit of money while we lived with Mrs. Baker, but not enough to pay the whole $7,200. My parents loaned me the rest of the money to buy the house, so we didn't have to go to a bank for a loan.

The house sits on Route 40-A, only about 600 feet from the church we were attending and where we were married. Every Saturday Mr. Newcomer came down to the church in the morning to walk and spend time with the Lord, and, afterward, he usually came to visit with Ruth and me.

The house we bought had been a post office and general store from 1842 to 1951. At one time, they'd even had gas pumps there. But the previous owner had died.

I had no interest in the store, which was in the basement of the house. The house was built into the side of a hill, and the basement had road frontage.

There was a cellar around in the back of the house, where I put in a water pump and a water heater. When we first moved in, there was a hand-dug well, which was only about fifteen feet deep, but it turned out to be no good. We drilled another well, but burned up a pump trying to get the water to clear up. After that, we drilled again, about 60 feet away, and this time we found good water. I also put in a new furnace, bought an electric stove (no wood stove for me), and purchased furniture.

Since we had plenty of room upstairs, we didn't use the storeroom area in the basement for many years. In fact, we lived in two rooms on the second floor and one room on the third floor and rented the rest of the second floor to Ruth's first cousin. I did a lot of work on the house. I removed two of the doors on the front and made them into windows, finding stones to match the rest of the house and doing the work myself. I cleaned all the concrete out of the cracks between the stones on the exterior walls of the house and had another man replace it, while I mixed the new concrete for him. This job, which would cost thousands of dollars today, cost me just $300 at the time.

We also put in a bathroom. There was a fairly large barn in back of the house, which I tore down, and we put in a driveway and built a 2-car garage. I also paid a mason to put a stone wall in, and I planted the hill in front of the house.

A lot of things happened in the 1950s. My brother Seibert bought a house in Boonsboro, and my Aunt Laura financed it for him. He also took the test to be an electrical contractor, so he could make some money on the side, and I worked with him. We worked two or three hours in the evenings. Later on, he quit his job at Potomac Edison and went into business for himself as an electrical contractor. He called his business Shifler Electric, and he did very well, employing up to 50 people. When I became an insurance agent, Seibert gave me all of the insurance business for his company and employees, and thus became one of my best policyholders. Seibert and his wife had four children, and I am still close to them all.

My brother, Woody, and his wife Jane got married in 1950, and he started tenant farming for different people, which he did for many years. Later in life, Woody delivered propane gas to people's homes and still did a lot of truck farming.

Luther, Ruth's brother, built a house in 1950, which cost him $10,000. He tried to get a job at the Fairchild aircraft plant, but when he took the physical, they told him he had a bad heart. He went to his local doctor in Boonsboro, and that doctor told him his heart was okay. After that, Luther went to work for the man who had been our Sunday school teacher. He started working there in the fall of 1955, and one night in February, 1956, he went to bed and never woke up. He died from a heart attack during the night.

In 1953, Ruth and I decided we wanted to have children, but she couldn't get pregnant. She went to her doctor and received treatment for this, and, finally, in 1955, our first child, Dale, was born. Our second son, Wayne, was born in 1957. All four of us slept in a bedroom on the third floor of the house.

Ruth worked until just before Dale was born, but after that she became a stay-at-home mom (other than filling in occasionally for the lady who had taken her job when she quit working at the Register of Wills office).

One Sunday in early 1956, our pastor, Curvin Thompson was preaching, and he told a story that was to have a profound impact on the remainder of my life, greatly affecting the way I related to everyone I met. He spoke about a potato farmer who had a huge pile of potatoes. He hired a man to come in and sort the potatoes into 1s, 2s, and 3s, according to their sizes. At the end of the day, the farmer asked the worker, "How do you like the job?"

The man answered, "Well, it isn't a bad job, but decisions, decisions, decisions!"

The minister concluded that our lives are a result of the decisions we have made in the past, and our future rests in the decisions we are now making and will make.

You Can't Outgive God

Pastor Thompson went on to tell us that the farmer gave ten percent of his big pile of potatoes away, and he couldn't see much difference in the pile after he had done it. He was using this story to teach us the principle of tithing. He said that we should take the tithe out of our paycheck first, and that way we wouldn't miss it as much. If we waited until after we paid our bills, it would be harder to do. God powerfully used that simple story to change the course of my life. When I heard it, I was married with a child, I was the only breadwinner in the family, and I was earning just $100 every other week. When my next paycheck came, I took out $10 and gave it to the church. The first time I did this, it did hurt, and I remember thinking, "How strange for me to do such a thing!" But the Bible says, *"Whatever a man sows, that shall he also reap"* (Galatians 6:7). On the farm, we could be sure that when we planted corn we would reap corn, and the harvest would be much more corn than we had planted. I began to plant money into the lives of other people, continuing to give away at least ten percent of my earnings. The Treasurer of our church once told me he couldn't understand how I could give away so much.

I thought it was amazing that out of all the great sermons I had heard over the years, God would use that simple story to change my life. When we hear a good sermon, we often say, "I'll never forget that one," but most times we do forget. Giving away money and helping other people has been a way of life for me ever since that day, and, as you will see, as my story progresses, you absolutely can't outgive God.

Soon after this, Pastor Thompson left Benevola and became the pastor of a larger church near Harrisburg, Pennsylvania, but he remained my close friend for the rest of his life.

My youngest brother, Charles, met a girl at the roller skating rink, and they were married in 1956. His wife worked for the state and had saved up some money. Charles asked the Doubs to sell him a building lot off the farm, and they sold him a lot on Millpoint Road. He built a house that cost about $10,000, and they moved into it in 1957. Charles continued working for our father and did a couple of other jobs around the area, until he finally got a job with the National Institute of Health in Washington, D.C. He worked there for 30 years, dissecting animals for research. Charles had only a high school education, but when he retired, they hired someone with a college degree to fill his position.

Charles never got farming out of his blood and always had a garden. He also raised turkeys and dressed them. When I bought the farm across from the Yellow House on Route 40-A, I sold him some ground, and he started raising steers. He killed about ten steers each year and sold the meat in halves or quarters.

My parents quit farming and sold their farm. In 1957, they bought seven acres up on Millpoint Road, which was only about half a mile from the farm. They built a house, a garage, a chicken house, a small smoke house, and a small barn. They raised chickens and steers, and they still butchered. But my dad no longer kept any horses after that, and, instead, bought himself a tractor.

Many times, my parents' house would get water in the basement, coming up through the concrete. I went to see the people who now own the house, and they said the water hasn't come up through the concrete for years, because the water table has gone down so much. Because of it, their well went dry, and they had to dig another one.

My father wasn't the best driver. He had the habit of looking out over the countryside while he was driving. One day my two sons, Dale and Wayne, were riding in the back seat, with my father at the wheel and my mother in the passenger seat beside the door. Dad wasn't watching where he was going and ran off the side of the road. He turned to Mom and said, "Damn, Ellen, if you hadn't been sitting so close to the door, I wouldn't have run off the road!" I thought it was humorous that he would try to blame his carelessness on my mother.

My parents stayed in that house on Millpoint Road for a long time. Daddy eventually developed Alzheimer's. One day he walked down to my brother Charles' house. They had a porch with no banisters around it, and Daddy fell off the porch. He had been smoking his pipe, and it was forced up through the roof of his mouth and killed him.

In time, Mom became a brittle diabetic, which is the most serious type. Her sugar sometimes went up to 600 or 700, and she perspired until her clothing was soaking wet. All five of us children lived close to her, and we would often go over and help her.

In 1982, Mom sold the house and divided all of the furniture between us children. To do this, she had each of us draw a number. The one who drew number 1 got first choice of the furniture, number 2 got second choice, and so forth until all five had chosen. Then she had us start with number 5, and that person got sixth choice, number 4 got seventh choice, and so forth back through number 1. We continued to follow this pattern and make selections until all the furniture was divided.

Eventually Mom had to go into Reeder Nursing Home in Boonsboro. In February, 1984, during a Valentine's Day Celebration, she was voted the "Queen of Hearts" at the nursing home and reigned over a week of activities that were held there. She won that honor by receiving the largest number of votes from her friends, who paid 10 cents a vote for the privilege. The money was then donated to the Arthritis Foundation.

Mom received a crown and a bouquet of red and white flowers and the honor of presiding over all of the festivities at the nursing home that week. She was a favorite among her friends there, because of her outgoing and friendly personality. There was a nice article in *The Daily Mail*, the Hagerstown newspaper, featuring a picture of our mother wearing her crown and holding her flowers.

CHAPTER SIX

JIM, THE METER READER

I had been working on this book for about five months, and was wondering what I should write about my first job as a meter reader with Potomac Edison some 64 years ago. Then, when I got the morning paper one morning, on the front page was an article with the caption in big letters: "METER READER SHORTAGE LEADS TO COMPLAINTS AGAINST UTILITY." How about that ... just when I was about to begin writing about this. As I noted at the outset, God does move in mysterious ways.

Here's what that newspaper article said:

> Potomac Edison, the electric provider for Western Maryland, has had difficulty retaining an adequate work force of meter readers, a company official said Friday. The shortage has caused complaints from some customers that they are being overcharged because Potomac Edison has failed to read meters as often as required. A formal complaint filed over the issue on May 21 [2012] by the Sugarloaf Conservancy of Frederick County,

Maryland, will be heard by the Public Service Commission on June 20, according to the PSC's tentative agenda.

Potomac Edison spokesman Todd Meyers said it's "unfortunate timing" that a complaint has been brought against the company because it has been actively recruiting additional meter readers to help alleviate problems. "We're making a full-court press here to get additional readers in," Meyers said.

"When meters cannot be read as scheduled each month, an estimate based on that month from the previous year is used for that billing cycle. But bills are 'trued up' when the next meter reading is taken," Meyers said.

"In some cases, meter readers are required to assist other Potomac Edison staff in helping restoration efforts after a significant outage, causing them to miss scheduled readings," Meyers said. "That's a challenge when you have meters needing to be read," he said.

State regulations allow for utility companies that bill on a monthly basis to estimate electricity usage every other billing month, as long as the utility provides customers the opportunity to read their own meters, which Potomac Edison does," Meyers said. "Readings by customers will be noted as an estimated reading on their bills," he said. Meyers said he is aware that a problem has existed, especially in the Frederick County area, due to large-scale job turnover and needed training for new employees.

"It's not optimal, but that's where we're at," he said. "It's been a challenge."

The article included a picture of a sign that said, "Now Hiring Meter Readers — Must have excellent driving record."

For years people told me they thought that reading meters was an easy job, but this article indicates otherwise. I would like to share with you some of the challenges presented by the job, from the perspective of one who has been there and done that.

One of the main problems I encountered was the dogs I came upon in the course of my duty. The ones I disliked the most were the little dogs. They would see me coming and run out, "Yap! Yap! Yap!" and try to bite at my feet. I couldn't kick them away because, if the customer had seen me kicking their dog, they would have been very upset, and I would have been in trouble.

Many times a female dog that had been friendly in the past would now have a litter of puppies, and this would make her cross because she was trying to protect her pups. Without warning, she would come out from under a bush and attack me. I was bitten by dogs seven times during my twelve-year career as a meter reader.

We had to read meters in all kinds of weather, cold or hot, rain, ice, or snow. I'll get to some more of those hardships later in the chapter.

On my first day on the job, I met the secretary in the office and discovered that she knew my family and was about the same age as my sister. There was an older man, who had been with the power company for many years. He did service work, fixed appliances, and climbed poles. I also met the man I was replacing. He had learned to climb poles and do service work, so he was moving up. I was happy when they said I wouldn't have to climb poles. My job was just to read meters and help with service work.

The man I was replacing was Gilbert Everline, but everyone called him "Buzzy." He and I were sharing something about ourselves, and when he told me his wife's name was Frankie, I was surprised because she was the daughter of one of our close neighbors, a man who used to thresh with us. We lived less than a mile apart, and she had ridden the same school bus I did, getting on and off at the very next stop.

When I went to work each morning, the first thing I did was review who on my route hadn't paid their electric bill (being careful to make sure they hadn't come in and paid it in recent days). If a bill was still unpaid, when I got to that house, I was required to cut off the service. Because the meters were not weatherproof in those days, they were often located inside the buildings. I had keys for those buildings, and as I came to them, I would unlock the door and go inside to read the meter. Later, when the meters were made to resist the weather, they were all relocated outside.

I had a meter book that was used to record the readings at each residence. This book was about twelve inches long and six inches wide, and it had a hard cover. It also came in handy for warding off pesky dogs. If they gave me too much trouble, I just threw the book at them.

There were no ball-point pens in those days, so I had to use a fountain pen to write down the meter readings. If it was raining or snowing, I would have to use the cover of the meter book to shield the ink from getting wet and smearing.

It was also my duty to subtract the previous reading from the new reading, to calculate exactly how much electricity had been used that period. This required many calculations each day. If the customer had a water heater, they had two meters (since there was a special electric rate for water heaters). In twelve years, no one ever complained about my subtraction, so I guess I didn't make too many mistakes.

You may have noticed in the accompanying newspaper article that the power company is now permitted to estimate the bill on alternate months and adjust it later when the meter is read. In our day, there was no such thing as estimating a bill. We read the meter faithfully every month.

One of the first things I had to learn, obviously, was how to read a meter. In those days a meter had 4 circles with numbers in them. Today there are five. Each circle was about

½ inch round and had the numbers 1 through 10 on them. The 10 was at the top, represented by a zero. There is a picture of a modern electric meter on page 118. With practice, I was able to glance at a meter and read all four numbers at the same time. I could read the meter by the position of the hands, much like looking at a clock and telling the time without actually seeing each number. I should have been good; I read about 2,500 meters a month for more than twelve years. Even today I can still stand fifteen feet from a meter and read it without glasses.

Before long, I was not just reading meters; they had me helping to deliver new appliances. Appliances were selling well, because many families had not bought them during the war. Now that the war was over, they were starting to buy again. To deliver an appliance, we took the truck that I used when I read meters, along with a dolly, so we didn't have to carry the appliance. When we delivered a refrigerator, we made sure it was level and demonstrated it to the customer, turning it off and on to make sure it worked. There was a salesman who worked out of Hagerstown, and he would go out and visit families' homes, and they also had an older lady who sometimes went out and demonstrated appliances.

If the appliance we were delivering and installing was a dryer, electric stove, or water heater, and the customer didn't have a 220-volt service to their house, we would install the upgrade free of charge. We did this, not only for the appliances we sold, but also for those everyone else sold.

This free service must have cost PE a lot of money, but it also brought them in some new business. Delivering an appliance and changing out the service took two men two to three hours to accomplish. PE had another truck, with a ladder and other special tools and supplies, used to do this work.

Before this, I had known nothing about electricity. My first day out, I was working with an older man, installing an appliance in the historic town of Sharpsburg. With 110-volt electrical services, there were two wires running into the house, but for 220, we had to put in three wires. First, we looked for a good spot to set the new meter and the new switch box. Most of the older homes had fuses, but these new switch boxes had breakers. We had to run all new wiring from the pole to the new meter and switch box.

The other man hooked up the wires on the pole and had me get up on the ladder and attach the wires going into the house. We had special connectors to tie it all together. He tied the new wires to the source on the pole, and I had to tie them to the service entrance at the top of the house. There was a technique for doing this without getting shocked, but he hadn't told me about that yet. So it would be correct to say that I had a shocking experience that day. After I got shocked, then the man taught me how to do it right.

When I started with PE, they had approximately 2,500 customers in the fifteen-mile radius around Boonsboro. Over the years, between reading meters and all the service work we did, I was in and around each family's house more than a hundred times. This helped me later, because I got to know a lot of people.

Buzzy stayed at PE until 1952. I went there in 1948, and we worked together a lot, delivering and installing appliances. He then left PE and worked at Fairchild for a while,

A modern electric meter

but later PE hired him back. Frankie and Buzz and Ruth and I became very good friends.

One time Buzz and I went out to hook up a range at a farmhouse. When we got there, the lady of the house was making cookies on a wood stove, and the range we were hooking up was behind the wood stove. She had a slop bucket full of food scraps sitting right there behind the wood stove, with no lid on it, and the whole two or three hours it took us to hook up the range we had to look at that slop bucket. When we were finished the job and about to leave, the lady said, "Would you like some of my cookies?" Buzz took some, but I said it might spoil my supper. Actually, it was the slop bucket that had spoiled my appetite.

Once I was out reading meters on a country road, and there was a poor elderly lady whose house wasn't very nice — and not very clean either. When I stopped to read her meter, she saw me coming. She came out of the house and said, "I just made a cake, and I'd like you to have a piece." I acted like I didn't want it, so she said, "Go ahead, it won't kill you." At the time, I wasn't too sure of that.

Another time Buzz and I were out installing an appliance, and we had finished and gotten in the truck to leave. The electric meter was on the front of the house, and I read it as we drove by, without us having to stop. Buzz had been a meter reader, and he hadn't believed I could do that. Some people got aggravated if I didn't get as close to their meter as they thought I should. They didn't realize that I could read their meter from quite a distance. They wanted to make sure I had read it correctly and that they weren't paying more than they should.

After having given all of this a lot of thought, I came to the conclusion that the problem was in the fact that electricity is invisible, and people don't think much about it unless and until it goes off. Most of the time, when someone does something, you can see it. The mailman brings you the mail, the milk man, in those days, brought the milk, and a bread man brought bread, but electricity was something that could not be seen, and yet they got a bill for it. This was unsettling and confusing for some.

Some people would hook up a heater or some other device that they imagined wouldn't use much electricity, and, then, when they got the bill, and it was higher than they expected, they thought I had read the meter wrong. One time a man came into our office and insisted that I had read his meter from 300 feet away. Another time a school teacher called and complained because I had gotten one wheel of the truck on her grass. Imagine, one wheel mark, and she called in and complained.

There was one house at Antietam Furnace near Sharpsburg where the house had a second floor porch, and that's where the meter was located. There were large railings to hold the porch up, but no steps, so I had to read that meter from 20 feet away. Once, over in Sharpsburg, I went to read the meter on a farm where there was a blind horse. When I opened the gate, there were no animals in sight, so I left the gate open. I had to go about 500 feet, and I knew it would only take a few minutes. While I was reading the meter, that horse approached and went out the open gate and headed for Sharpsburg. I had to follow him into Sharpsburg in the truck until I caught him. Then I walked back, leading the horse out to the farm and put him in the gate. Then I had to walk back into town and get my truck to continue my rounds.

When I went to read the meter on a farm with a gate, it required that I get in and out of the truck three times just to read that one meter. It was a lot of extra work, just to open and close that gate.

One man saw that I was coming to read his meter and, instead of letting me in the open gate, he shut the gate and made me get in and out of the truck.

There was a meter located near the river, and I had to climb a hundred steps to get close enough to read it, and I did that once every month. If fact, in our book, there were three places down by the river that had a lot of steps, and I had to read all those meters the same day. That was a lot of extra steps. When I took my vacations, I always made sure the person who was filling in for me read those meters that month.

While I was working at Potomac Edison, they required each of us to work one weekend a month in the office — three hours on Friday night and all day on Saturday. During those hours, people came into the office to pay their bills, shop for appliances, or register complaints. Oh, how I hated working in the office! To me, it made for a long, boring day, and it was like torture to me. I also had to count the money, checking it in at the beginning of the day and checking it out at the end. Many times, just when I was ready to close and go home, someone would come in and want to talk, so I was delayed in getting home. I much preferred my work in the field.

I had many strange experiences while reading meters. One time I went into a lady's yard to read the meter, and she had covered the meter with her panties. I had to take them off to read the meter. I never did figure out what *that* was all about.

Another time, in a little village, there was a house with a side porch. As I rounded the corner of the house to read the meter, I came upon a lady squatting and urinating on the porch. Of course, I was shocked and surprised, but all I could think of to say was, "Hello." I certainly hadn't been expecting anything like that. She was also startled by my appearance, and she got up and tried unsuccessfully to pull her dungarees up, but she couldn't get them up fast enough. In the end, she hurried into the house with her bare bottom still sticking out.

As I was reading meters one day, I stopped at a local country store run by an older lady and her son. I never snacked much, but I had stopped that day to get a bottle of soda pop or a candy bar. When I went in, there was a young kid in the store. He got a candy bar, took the wrapper off, and threw the wrapper on the floor. The older lady said to him, "Do you do that at home?"

The kid answered, "Yeah."

The lady replied, "Well, make yourself at home." At least there was a little humor in the job.

As I noted before, part of my job was to turn people's lights off when they didn't pay their bill. Sometimes they got angry with me, even though I was just doing my job. Once, I had turned off a fellow's lights over on the Sharpsburg Pike. He came in and paid his bill, so they sent me back out to turn the lights back on. While I was out of my truck, turning his lights on, he got in his car and pulled in back of me and wouldn't let me out of his driveway. I had to call the State Police to get out of there.

After I had been with PE for many years, a maintenance man complained that they were spending too much money for my vehicle repair and maintenance, and he thought maybe I was a bad driver. He called me one day and said he wanted to go along with me to make my rounds. I thought, "Okay, I'll fix him!"

I drove around normally most of that day, but then we came to a place way up in the mountains, where there was a very steep hill to go up. Even though it was summertime, I knew it was impossible for that light truck to climb the hill. I always got out and walked. I got out now and told the man I would like for him to drive up the hill. He got behind the wheel and tried his best to take the truck up the hill, but he soon saw that it just couldn't be done. After that day, he never again complained about my driving.

I had to cut off one man's electric service twice, and each time he reconnected it himself. When the third time came, the company sent someone out to disconnect the high tension wire that ran from the transformer to the house, so he was unable to turn the service back on by himself.

The funniest story I can remember was about a lady in Appletown, down below Boonsboro. I had turned her lights off, and the next month when she saw me coming to read the meter she wouldn't let me in her yard. There was a fence about ten feet from the meter, so I walked on the other side of the fence and read the meter from there without any problem. The next month, she had a broom and wouldn't let me get close enough to the fence to read the meter at all. Our manager had to go out and straighten the woman out.

You might be surprised to learn that when someone suffered a power outage, I would often be called out to fix it, even though I was just a humble meter reader. This happened quite often in my twelve years with the company.

One winter there was a big snow storm, and it caused a lot of wires to be pulled loose from the houses and knocked lines out on the road. In some cases, it had pulled the entrance cable loose from the house, and so the family had no electricity. Potomac Edison asked my brother Seibert and me to go out and restore service to these houses. We worked about three days in the snow and cold weather, restoring people's power.

I also worked as a "ground man" when we went out to install appliances. There was a rope hanging down from the man on the pole, and if he needed something, I would attach it to the rope and send it up to him. One Christmas Day I was eating lunch with my family when I received a call that a transformer had burned up. Buzz and I went out and worked all afternoon, putting up a new transformer.

Another time, Buzz and I were out working during a storm. The storm was almost over, and Buzz had climbed the pole, when suddenly lightening struck nearby. I have never seen the sky light up like that. I called up, "Buzz, are you still up there?" Thankfully, he was okay.

Potomac Edison was a good place to work, and they were always very fair with us workers. When I was called out to turn someone's lights on, it may have taken me only a short period of time, but they paid me for three hours work. For longer jobs, after the three hours, we got time and a half, so that was very generous. We also got a week's paid vacation each year, health insurance, and retirement benefits.

During the time I worked for PE, I was chosen to be on the Federal Grand Jury in Baltimore. They paid me a fee per day to serve, and PE made up the difference in my pay. One of the other jurors lived in Western Maryland, and so we drove down to Baltimore together. We served on the jury for three months, and I really enjoyed hearing the cases. This was in the 1950s, and a lot of the cases involved people who were selling moonshine.

While I was working for the power company, there were two occasions when I could have accidentally killed a child. The first one was out at Mapleville. I was driving the power company truck, and as I was going in Mapleville Road, a young girl ran out in front of me. I had to think fast. If I had veered to the right, I would have hit a big tree and a house. I chose to swing the truck to my left instead.

The truck had metal sides that we tied the appliances to, when we delivered them. I caught the girl with the back end of the truck, and her arm or shoulder was broken. When the police came, however, they were not very sympathetic. They asked me why I hadn't steered the truck to the right toward the tree and the house, gave me a ticket, and said I had to appear in court.

As I thought back over the happening, I remembered a bus that was going in the opposite direction. I was able to locate the bus driver, and he went to court with me. They said that I must have been speeding, but the bus driver testified that I was not speeding and that I was driving safely. Consequently, all charges were dropped.

The other occasion was equally as frightening. I went back a long farm lane to a house on the right. I turned left, to turn the truck around and position it so I could get out on the driver's side and read the meter. When I tried to pull forward, the steering wheel of the truck just spun. On the farm, when driving in a field, this would happen if I hit a rock, so I got out and took a look. I was shocked to find a young boy, about six years old, pinned against my front wheel. If I had continued forward, I would have crushed him.

I got in the truck and backed up so he could get out, and he got up and ran away. Completely shaken by the experience, I went to the house and told the child's mother what had happened. I was relieved when she responded, "It serves him right. He's always running after vehicles." She said she would take him to the doctor and have him checked out, but I never heard anything more from them. If that happened today, I would probably be facing a big law suit.

In looking back over my life, these two events stand out to me as times when God Almighty protected me from tragic disasters that would have altered the entire course of my future. I wish to give sincere thanks and praise to Him for His mercy and grace.

CHAPTER SEVEN

JIM SHIFLER, INSURANCE AGENT

When I started tithing, I always looked for the best way to help people. Potomac Edison also encouraged us to take an active part in the community. About that time, I happened to see an article in the newspaper about the United Fund, which was raising money for a number of charitable organizations in Washington County. I remember thinking to myself, "What a good way to support these organizations! Instead of sending out workers from each charity, they have joined together to raise money for all of them." That's how I got involved with the United Fund. I called them and said I would like to give them a donation. Little did I know that, by doing this, I had opened the door to later becoming an insurance agent.

Potomac Edison gave us time off from work to give blood, which I did for many years, even after I no longer worked for PE. Altogether, in more than fifty years, I gave twenty-three gallons of blood. In fact, I continued to do this until they wouldn't allow me to give anymore, because of the medications I was taking. I always thought it was fun to give blood, and I did it at various places, even while we were away on vacations. One lady who was taking my blood told me, "My, you have beautiful veins."

I also got involved in collecting donations for the United Fund. It was my job to collect money in the Benevola area and at our church, now Benevola United Methodist. There was one lady who gave me a donation of $400 each year, which was a lot of money, and that made me look good as a collector.

One day in 1958 I came home for lunch, and John Brady, the district sales manager for Nationwide Insurance, was waiting to see me. He asked me if I could find a chairman for the United Fund for each of the little towns in the south part of Washington County (twelve in total). He said he had called someone in Boonsboro, and they told him, "Get Jim Shifler to do it."

Even though I had been doing some volunteer work with the United Fund, this turn of events has always been a mystery to me. First of all, why would this man call someone in the little town of Boonsboro, where only a couple of thousand people lived? And I didn't even live in Boonsboro. Who did he call? And why did they recommend me? I never knew. Anyway, I agreed to help him.

My responsibility was to find a person to be a chairman in each of those little towns, and of course, I knew people in all of them because I had been reading their meters for a long time. I found the twelve chairmen needed, took the literature out to them and then went back and picked up the money they collected. The people I had chosen did a good job, and John Brady was very pleased.

Mr. Brady next asked me if I might consider becoming an insurance agent. I had thought I might like being a salesman, but I had never thought about selling insurance. I said, "I'll try it." He told me that first I would have to take a personality test. He didn't seem to be interested in how smart I was, just in whether I had the right personality to be an agent. The personality test results indicated that I would be a good agent, and that's how I got the job.

As my district sales manager, Mr. Brady gave me a book to study to prepare for my licensing. I read and studied that little book, and Mr. Brady quizzed me, to see if I was ready for the exams. That's how I got my education to sell insurance. When Mr. Brady was confident that I could pass, I went to Baltimore and took the test for my insurance license.

There were three different tests I had to take. The first one was on casualty insurance, which included fire, automobile, and commercial. The second test was on selling life and health insurance, and the third, which I took later, was the hardest of all. It was the stockbroker's test, which was necessary because Nationwide also sold mutual funds. I actually did better on the stockbroker's test than I did on the other two, simply because I worked the hardest to learn the material. There was a lot of technical language involved, and some of the other men had to take the test two or three times to pass it. My score, the first time around, was 86.

One of the things I had studied really paid off. About two years before this, we had lost our garage. We were accustomed to burning our trash in a nearby field, and one Sunday we came home from church and decided to lie down in the afternoon and take a nap. While we were sleeping, the fire ran up the field and burned our garage down. Thinking that I didn't have insurance on the garage, just the house, I had never pursued the matter. Now I learned that when you purchase a homeowner's policy, any outbuildings are covered for ten percent of the value of the house. I called the insurance company, and they paid me for my garage.

I got my license in December of 1959, but I didn't start selling insurance until about the middle of the following year. Even though I sold no insurance in 1959, when they counted how long I had been an agent, they always counted that year, even though I hadn't gotten my license until that December.

The easy part was passing the tests; now I had to learn how to sell insurance. At first Mr. Brady went out with me on my visits. He assigned me to get prospects. For instance, on one occasion, he asked me to find prospects for health insurance, so I made a list of people I knew who were not in good health. When he saw that, he said, "Damn it, Jim, if you're going to be an insurance agent, you will have to learn how to prospect." That really helped me. With those few words, he had given me a one-line crash course in prospecting. Some agents did very little prospecting, but that one simple statement made more of a lasting impression on me than if I had studied for many hours in a classroom.

Another time we were out trying to sell a policy, and he was impressed with the way I had handled myself and the things I had said to the customer. That's when he told me that he had been a coach at Brunswick High School. He said, "Jim, there was a young man who played ball for me. He didn't look like a ball player, and he didn't act like a ball player, but he knew how to score, and that's the way you are." So that's how I got my training. In 1987, when I retired from insurance, it cost $50,000 to train a new agent. It's probably much more than that today.

Soon I had to decide where I would locate my office. Mr. Brady had brought me fifty policies from a previous agent in a cardboard box, and since I didn't even have a filing cabinet, I was working out of that box. Ruth's cousin, who had rented from us, had moved out by that time. So, since we now had an extra room in our house, we decided to put the insurance office right there.

It wasn't a very handy place for an office. From Route 40-A, people had to come up twenty-three steps and then walk the whole way around to the back of the house and enter through one of those foot-and-a-half thick doorways. When they stepped through that door, they were in a room twenty feet long and eight feet wide, and as they entered, my

Our first home and office on Route 40-A

desk was first, and another desk sat behind that, which was for my future secretary. The room was also large enough for our filing cabinets (once we got some) and a little stand for a typewriter. Since Ruth was answering the phone and typing up my policies, that's all the overhead I had. I put in a nice driveway about 50 feet behind the house, but most people didn't use it. They continued to come up the steps and around the side of the house, and I never remember anyone complaining about the inconvenience. This always amazed me — especially since our office remained in that place for the next eighteen years.

Sometimes people try to give you helpful advice, when they really don't understand anything about your background or your personality. This happened to me back in 1959, when I first became an agent. Another agent said to me, "Jim, never go out to see a client unless you can make at least $10 on that call." Now, $10 was a good bit of money in 1959. I made lots of calls, even when I knew I wouldn't make any money at all on them. That same man told me, "Jim, never sell to farmers; I can't understand them." Maybe he couldn't understand them, but I was one of them, so I could. When he said that, he probably didn't know that I had been born and raised on a farm. That was definitely not good advice for me, because farmers became some of my best clients in the years ahead.

One day I was surprised by a call from Aunt Laura. She had called to say that she had married, and she and her new husband, Leonard Schlosser, wanted to give me their car insurance. It was my first policy. Aunt Laura was about 62 years old when she married Leonard. He had accidentally cut off his hand (using a saw, just like the one we boys had used to saw our wood into pieces for the wood stove), so he had a metal hook where his hand had been. The two of them traveled, and Aunt Laura enjoyed life with Leonard and enjoyed being married. Aunt Laura was a wonderful lady with a very pleasing personality. She had been very good to my parents, lending them money to go into farming, and also to my brother, lending him money to buy his house.

When she was 75 years old, Aunt Laura was honored by her church, Mt. Nebo Evangelical Brethren, for having taught the Men's Sunday School Class for fifty years. In 1912, she had agreed to take over a class of small boys, who were now men in their fifties (at the time she was honored in 1962). Others later joined the class, which had as many as forty members at a time, and she had an estimated total of a hundred and fifty students over the fifty years. She also served as the church organist and directed plays and pageants at the church.

When Aunt Laura died, my brother was the executor of her will, and he sold the house and furniture. Leonard went into a nursing home, and I was surprised to be given the power of attorney to take care of him. When I started handling Leonard's money, he had $24,000 in his checking account, which wasn't drawing any interest at all. At that time, you could invest money for three years and get a seventeen percent return. Leonard was a very nice fellow and easy to get along with, so this was no burden to me. At one point, they called me and asked me to come, because he was in the hospital. The doctors wanted to put a pacemaker in, and the first thing Leonard wanted to know was if he could afford it. He wasn't interested in what it would do for him, just in knowing if he could afford it.

I didn't know how I would be reimbursed for taking care of Leonard, so I decided to take $500 a year for my services. When he died, his accountant and I worked on his estate, instead of getting a lawyer involved. He was now worth $460,000. I put in a bill to the Orphan's Court for $1,000, for my part in settling up the estate, and they couldn't get over the fact that this was all I charged.

Leonard left a large amount of money to charity, and I knew the remainder of his money was to be divided between six of us, which included my sister and brothers, one of our first cousins, and myself. It resulted in a nice sum for each of us.

CHAPTER EIGHT

IMPORTANT DECISIONS

When I first started selling insurance, my best friend said to me, "Jim, you'll never make it as an insurance salesman because you don't talk enough," but I have learned that many times being a good listener is more important than being a good talker. I have known many I thought would make it because they were good talkers, but if you don't have the other characteristics it takes to be a successful insurance agent, you won't make it.

After two and a half years, I was making as much money selling insurance part time as I was making working for the power company full time and one day the Regional Vice President of Nationwide came up from Annapolis (our state capitol) to talk to me about going full time with them. In my mind, there was just one drawback. I remembered how miserable I had been sitting in that office at PE on Friday evenings and Saturdays once a month. I thought, "How am I going to be an insurance agent, when I don't like sitting in an office?"

I also considered that while working for Potomac Edison I had paid vacation time, and they also paid for my health insurance, and contributed to my retirement benefits. With Nationwide, I would be self-employed and, other than a retirement program, I would have to pay everything myself. Even with those drawbacks, going full time with Nationwide was the smartest move I ever made. With them, I got a good education in business, and I loved working with people, and truly enjoyed selling insurance.

Sitting in an office didn't turn out to be my style as an insurance agent. Instead, I got to the office early and took care of anything that needed my attention. Then I left the office and went out to visit people, and that's how I built up my business.

The personality test was right. I never dreamed I could sell insurance, but I had all the qualities that it took to be a good agent. Years later, after I had retired, I had an opportunity to take another personality test at our church. It was called the Myers-Briggs Type Indicator and consisted of at least a hundred questions. After answering these questions, the information was analyzed. Guess what it said about me? I scored high in extraversion, sensing, thinking, and judging. This meant that I am practical, realistic, matter of fact, and have a natural head for business or mechanics.

The test further indicated that I am not interested in subjects I see no use for, but I can apply myself to them when necessary. I like to organize and run activities. It also said that I would make a good administrator, especially if I remember to consider others' feelings and points of view. I wish I had known all of these things about myself earlier in life. This test must have been very similar to the one John Brady gave me when I became an insurance agent.

There were many things I had learned on the farm growing up that helped me become a good insurance agent. On the farm, we had to get up at 5:30 or 6:00 A.M., to milk the cows, and we would work until about 7 o'clock at night in the busy season.

Because of this, I learned to work long hours. So going out two nights a week to sell life insurance was no problem for me. When I compared the amount of work involved in selling insurance with that involved in farming, I thought, "How did I get such an easy job?"

Before I had become an insurance agent, I had often seen articles in the newspaper rating the reputation of those in different professions. Used car salesmen and insurance salesmen always had the worst rating in those days. I decided, right from the start, that I would never do anything that would give insurance agents a bad name. One of the men who worked for me later took over my agency, and his secretary told me, after I retired, that out of all the agents around, no one had ever complained to her about me.

One time a man asked me for a quote on auto insurance. I gave him a quote, and so did another company. I knew my price should be as good as the other agent's, but it turned out that his quote was lower, so he got the policy. I decided to go see how he had quoted a better rate than I had. What I learned was that he had left some coverage off of the policy, and that's how he had beat me. It was terrible what some agents did to sell insurance, and that's how they got such a poor reputation.

I always had my office open on Saturday morning, even though none of the other agents did. A funny thing happened one day at the office. As people would come up the steps to pay their premiums, Ruth and I would question each other as to who should take care of them. Sometimes it was more convenient for one or the other of us. This day, when we heard someone coming, I asked her if I should take care of it, but she said, "I'll take this one."

It was a lady and she had come to pay her bill. During the course of the conversation, she told Ruth about an operation she had just undergone and actually pulled up her dress and pulled down her pants to show Ruth her incision. After the lady left, Ruth told me what had happened. "You should have taken that one," she said. "You missed the boat."

An older man who lived in Boonsboro but attended our church, wanted health insurance for himself and his wife, so I sold him an individual health policy for the two of them. When I started selling insurance, the hospital room rate was $5 per day, plus an amount for the medications and other expenses. When his wife later died, he learned that the drugs used to treat her had cost more than $600. His comment was, "Well, no wonder she died, if they gave her all that medicine!" Selling insurance had its comical moments.

I mentioned in an earlier chapter about some of the games I played when I was growing up, and how I was always trying to figure out the shortest and best way to do things. I had always believed that no matter how many times you have done something, you might still find another way that is faster or better. I loved to find shortcuts, but I made sure that they didn't sacrifice the quality of my work. During my career, I had four different district sales managers. At my retirement, the last one said, "Jim, you have found a way to do things quicker than anyone I have ever seen and still do it right."

As an agent I employed a principle I had first used when playing basketball and soccer in high school. Scoring a basket or a goal had always been very exciting for me, and that's the same way I felt about selling insurance. When I sold someone a policy I knew would really help them, I got excited, not about making the money, but about being able to help someone. To me it was like scoring a winning basket.

As the business grew, I found that even though Ruth typed up policies and answered the phone, I needed someone who could manage the office when the two of us went away on a trip. When we moved into the house we purchased on Route 40-A, there was an older lady living next door named Blanche Wyand. She had chickens, and she wasn't able to care for them, so I would feed and water them for her.

You Can't Outgive God

The chickens were so old that they never laid eggs. When Blanche died, her property, including the house, barn and land, was to be sold in front of the court house. Ruth wanted us to buy it, but her first cousin, Danny Baker, and his wife, Doris, also wanted it. I told Ruth, "We already have a place, so let them buy it." I knew that property was a good investment, but I had made my decision, and I stood by it.

The day of the sale I didn't go to bid on the property, but another first cousin of Danny's did. She also owned property near Blanche's, and she was convinced this would be a good investment. It was a nice piece of land, with two or three buildings on it, and it sold that day for only $3,800 (that was in May of 1966). Danny and Doris Baker got it.

Doris had worked for another insurance company, and so now I hired her to help us. As I began to write this book and to think back over the things that had happened in my life, I realized that if I had bought that piece of property, I never would have hired Doris as my secretary, and she became a tremendous asset to the business.

At first, Doris said she could only work three hours a day, but later she decided to work four, from 8 A.M. to 12 NOON, but she could accomplish more in those four hours than most other secretaries could in a full eight-hour day. I never remember her bringing anything to work to eat or drink. All of her time there was spent working, and she did a wonderful job. She also learned to write auto and fire insurance, which took some of the load off of me. I definitely see this as God at work again.

That property came up for sale just when I needed a secretary. Doris worked for me for more than twenty years, and she also did my bookkeeping, my quarterly reports, paid the bills, and took care of everything else that needed to be done around the office. She was truly instrumental in my success as an insurance agent.

Danny, Doris' husband, was also a blessing. He had a tractor and plowed the snow from the front of my house so people could park their cars when they came to the office. He was also a very good carpenter and handy in other ways. He helped me with lots of different projects.

Many years later, Doris suffered a stroke. As she was recovering, the doctor asked Danny where she had worked. It seems that all Doris could talk about was getting back to work, and the doctor felt that her desire to do that was probably what kept her alive and was responsible for her recovery. Doris did get back to work and also lived to enjoy her retirement. She just passed away about two years ago.

CHAPTER NINE

GOOD FRIENDS AND GOOD TIMES

In 1961 a young minister named Charles Lightner and his wife, Harriet, came to our church to serve as our new pastor. They stayed at Benevola for the next ten years and became our close friends. I thought it would be very interesting for him to tell you about our great friendship. We have known each other for 52 years. The following are some memories he wrote down, at my request, to include in this book:

MEMORIES ABOUT JAMES SHIFLER

Upon graduation in 1961 from United Theological Seminary in Dayton, Ohio, my superintendent informed me that I would be assigned to a newly-formed appointment in some places in Maryland I'd never heard of called Benevola and Mt. Lena — two United Methodist churches that had been separated from Boonsboro Church in Maryland.

Benevola was primarily a farming community and Mt. Lena a basic blue-collar one of folks who worked in Hagerstown. I visited all of the members of the two congregations, and one of those visits was the U.S. Route 40-A home of Jim and Ruth Shifler. They and their two sons, Dale and Wayne, made us feel right at home, and our shared fondness for that egregious vice, Bridge, made us most sympathetic to one another. Since we thought it might be nice to continue to talk to our mates after a Bridge evening, we determined, from the very outset, that the men would compete against the women, so peace could reign in our respective homes after the night's card table wars. Whoever said Bridge was a genteel game has not played husbands against wives. It's a dog-eat-cat fight, as soon as the first card's played. And if you ever want to play with a Master without papers, play with Jim. It's a blood-sport with no quarter given — particularly to two wives who'd brag about it that night or the next morning. Of course, Jim (Gentleman Jim) and I were always respectful of the ladies and would never mention again how we thrashed them on the sacred table of honor. By the way, these serene moments of blood-letting would take place after holy music had been sung at choir practice that evening.

Harriet and I would dress up our two little ones in their sleepers, carry them up to the Shifler's, and nestle them in Jim and Ruth's big bed on the ground floor, and away they'd float to netherland, while we'd wrestle with hearts and spades into the wee hours. Did we warp the little buggers in some unknown way? Otherwise it was a very beautiful and bucolic life there in bountiful Benevola.

Then, again, the United Methodist Church called, and we were sent away to a new church in St. Charles, Maryland, south of Washington, D.C. But we had to keep up our Bridge to each other. So I can recall clearly one night meeting Ruth and Jim at the old Washingtonian Hotel on the Interstate. We had a lovely supper and, when asked what room we might go to play the night's game, were told by the manager that it could not be done in the hotel's bounds, although if we'd rent a room, we could use the "play" room of the hotel for card playing. We looked at each other and wandered outside to the parking lot and lo, a bright light struck us. We went to the hotel's dumpster and hauled out a suitably-sized cardboard box for a table and then dragged two benches off the hotel's golf course, and played to our hearts' content into the morning hours under a parking lot light. It's what one does when thwarted!

James and I would play game after game of HORSE or CAT in the curving drive of his home, where he'd placed a legal hoop for basketball (just above his highly prized garden). These, too, were hard-fought competitive encounters between two otherwise "sweet" gentlemen. And did I mention: Benevola Church had a softball team that played other churches in the area? Gentleman Jim was our pitcher, and he was a darn good one.

We won that church league several times in the eight years I was there, and Jim was always our pitcher. A crowning achievement was playing in a Donkey Softball game or two while there. Jim had to pitch with one hand and hold on to the "jackass" with another. We all had to either be on our donkeys or holding onto them. Try fielding a ball in your environs with a donkey that had no more interest in pursuing that rolling ball than the man-in-the-moon. Fact is, it was fun for all, if you didn't mind being laughed at a lot. Those donkeys could sure humble a guy.

Speaking of humbling, Jim and I played golf at the Muni course in Hagerstown, and I would, in later years, join him for a game or two on the Beaver Creek Course, where Jim has held a membership for some time. I still buy Titlist Pro VI balls from Jim, who, in his retired years, roams the area's golf courses, picks up wayward balls, sells them, and gives the profits to his favorite charities. Thanks to him, I'll never run out of golf balls to lose.

One of the most infamous trips Ruth, Jim, Harriet and I took was to Rehoboth Beach on a national holiday — which we just up and did one summer on a whim, without making reservations. "We'll have no trouble getting a room," we men told our less-than-confident wives. When we got there, we went to every motel/hotel we could see and always we got the same refrain: "Sorry, we're all full up. You should have made a reservation!" Finally we found a so-called "Tourist Home," at which we inquired and, yes, they had rooms for rent. This was like a venture into the Rue Morgue. There was only one forty-watt bulb in each room and the bed, chest, and drapes were all of a heavy, dark, depressing flavor. It was as though it was "Psycho" all over again! Any minute, you were sure Tony Perkins would arrive, dagger in hand and end us all! No matter how long the trip down was, it was not a night for Morpheus!

Somewhere along the line, Jim was asked by the Nationwide folks to consider taking the place of an area insurance salesman who was retiring. Jim and I talked about it, and he talked with others, I'm sure, because he had a good job with Potomac Edison as a meter reader — which, if you think about it, got Jim into most of the homes in Boonsboro and the surrounding areas. So he knew most of the people living there. He made the right decision, and I don't think he ever looked back. And he became a Nationwide Hall of Famer.

But Jim was already in Harriet's and my Hall of Fame, because we had looked for years for a proper home to call our own. We'd looked in Maryland, Virginia, and West Virginia. Then, one day, sitting at our parents' home in Pennsylvania, we saw an ad for a place in Caledonia, between Gettysburg and Chambersburg, just off Route 30. We went, we saw, and we wanted it. But how? They demanded a lot of money down for good faith, to hold the property. What could we do? We were earning only $1,700 a year, so we went to Jim and asked him to loan us the money until we could arrange a bank loan through our parents. That was 1970, and he cheerfully loaned us a large sum of cash (with no interest involved). We paid him back in a few weeks, and from then until now we still have a lovely second home in Caledonia. Thank you, Jim and Ruth!

Good Friends and Good Times

Charlie and Harriet are still great friends with our family until this day. When he served two other churches, in Saint Charles, Maryland, and Bel Air, Maryland, we would try to go to his worship service on a Sunday to hear him preach a good sermon, even though one of the churches was eighty miles away. Then we would visit together in the afternoon. When Charlie retired from the Bel Air Church, he had three associate pastors. After his retirement, the church built a new library building and named it after him.

Whenever Charlie and Harriet come back to Caledonia, where they still have a cabin, they always make a visit to Boonsboro, usually once or twice a year. He has now retired to Maine, but he still comes back to see his two daughters. One of them lives below Washington, D.C., and the other lives in southern Maryland. And when he comes to see them, he also stops to see us. In fact, he has been here three times already this year. When I celebrated my 80th birthday, Charlie made a special trip from Maine to attend the party. He's asking us to go to Maine for a visit, but I told him my Maine days are over.

I had another friend named Lehman Toms, who liked to play cards, and I taught him to play 500. The next time we were together, I said, "Let's play a game, just for fun, to get started." I played one card twice, and the other three people playing didn't seem to notice it. We were already in the next hand, when Lehman said, "By Ganny, Jim, you cheated that last hand! You played a card twice!"

You Can't Outgive God

My laughing reply was, "My, you're a fast thinker!"

Lehman liked to take risks and would bid even when he had nothing in his hand. It is my observation that men are more aggressive than women, when it comes to playing cards.

Through the years I enjoyed taking an active part in the community. I served as president of the PTA at the Boonsboro Elementary School. My two sons never played baseball, but one day a man from the Little League in Boonsboro came to see me. He said they couldn't find anyone willing to be president of the Little League and would I please become the president? I went to the first meeting, and learned that the only person running was a woman. I guess they didn't want a woman to be their president, so I told them I would run. They held the election, and I became the president of the Little League. I did that for a couple of years, and then had to tell them I was too busy to continue, but I gave them a nice check to build a fence, so I left on a high note.

One of the teachers in the high school asked me to come each year and talk to his students about insurance. The teacher didn't have any insurance with me, and I could never understand why he asked me, rather than his own insurance agent, but I went and gave a talk once a year for several years. Since the students were about the age to get their driver's license, I gave them a detailed talk about automobile insurance. I never did ask that teacher to buy insurance from me.

Good Friends and Good Times

After my sons got out of high school, I was asked to become part of a committee to sit in with the members of the Board of Education and talk about problems in the school. They were looking for someone from the community to participate, so I served on that committee for a few years. Besides all these activities, I still remained active in our church.

All of this was done in my spare time, after spending my days and some of my evenings selling insurance. I have now been retired for twenty-four years, and I still have people saying that they miss me and that they liked the way I conducted my insurance business.

CHAPTER TEN

CHANGES

John Brady, my district sales manager, treated me like a son. Because I did well selling insurance, I won trips, which meant that he, as my district sales manager, also got to take trips, and sometimes we traveled together.

I was pleased that our insurance business kept growing, and in 1967 I was surprised when someone called to say that our agency had made President's Club. This meant that we were in the top three percent in sales in the entire company. To qualify for this, you also had to have a good loss ratio. At the beginning of each year, the company sent us the goals we were to accomplish, and I made them without even knowing I was making them. Mr. Brady was so excited about us making President's Club that he took all the agents in the district and their wives to the Red Byrd Restaurant to celebrate.

For making President's Club, Nationwide gave us a trip to Colorado Springs. Wherever we went, they would fly us and provide us with excellent accommodations and meals. While we were in Colorado Springs, we visited the Air Force Academy and saw all the beautiful rock formations. Mr. Brady and his wife were also with us on that trip.

You Can't Outgive God

We also saw Royal Gorge Bridge, which, at a thousand feet high, is the highest bridge in the United States. When Ruth and I were walking across the bridge, we were surprised to meet a lady we knew, Doris Haynes from Gapland, Maryland. It certainly is a small world. In my travels I have often come across people from back home. This happened at the Statue of Liberty in New York, at Disney World in Florida, and even when flying home from England. We met a man we knew from Keedysville, Maryland.

Once, in Bermuda, we were talking to another of our Hall of Famers and his wife. They shared with us throughout an evening the story of their daughter losing her husband and then traveling overseas to take his ashes. While flying home, we had a connecting flight from Philadelphia to Baltimore. When my wife and I got on the plane, who should board the plane and sit next to us, but the very daughter they had been telling us about!

At the end of 1968, I learned that I had made President's Club again, and this time we went to Florida. We took our two sons along that time. We were all invited on a moonlight cruise and our sons, Dale and Wayne, were excited about going. Ruth and the boys got on the ship, but I was with the Bradys, and we left a little later. Imagine our surprise when we discovered that there were actually two ships, and I was on the wrong one. Instead of going on a moonlight cruise with my lovely wife and our sons, I ended up on a cruise with my district sales manager and his wife!

The following year we won a cruise that was to leave from New York. We were on our way there by car to board the ship. There was a large gasoline tank truck in the right lane, and I was driving our vehicle in the left-hand lane. Suddenly, without warning, the driver of the gasoline truck cut right in front of me, to turn into a gas station on my left. To keep from hitting him and to avoid a terrible accident, I turned and drove our vehicle right beside the gasoline truck, also turning into the gas station. Otherwise we would have gone underneath the tank trailer and most likely been killed. Mr. Brady and his wife were in the back seat, and she was amazed that I'd had the reaction to do this. We were shaken up a

With Ruth about 1969

bit but not physically injured. Again, to God be the glory!

One year Jack Brady and I wanted to attend the World Series. I sent money to buy tickets, but each time it was returned. Apparently you had to have political connections to get tickets to the World Series. Brooks Robinson was playing for the Baltimore Orioles at the time, and they had made it to the World Series, so we really wanted to go.

We had a regional sales manager named Bill Corrigan, who had been a professional ball player before he became a Nationwide agent. I called him, and he got me tickets to the World Series. Jack and I really enjoyed that game, and we got to see Brooks Robinson make some wonderful plays. He was later inducted into the Baseball Hall of Fame.

Bill Corrigan later changed jobs with Nationwide and took over another agency. He did very well and sold a lot of insurance. In fact, he, too, is in the Nationwide Hall of Fame.

In 1970 the Nationwide agents in the Hagerstown area experienced a big change. My dear friend Jack Brady retired as district sales manager. He and his wife, however, remained close friends with us for many years. One Christmas they got a live tree, and after Christmas had passed, they gave it to us. We were leaving for a six-week stay in Florida, so we put that tree down in our basement and watered it. Then, when we got back, we planted it in our yard. That tree is now thirty feet tall. Another time Mrs. Brady gave us a beautiful handmade afghan.

Mr. Brady taught me a lot about insurance, and when I did well, I became his pride and joy. In his later years, he would sometimes call and ask me questions about his own insurance. His son lived up near Boston, so I guess he wasn't always there to help out. It felt rather strange, when I looked at how things had changed. He had been my teacher, and now I was answering his questions.

When Mr. Brady retired, a young man named Ralph May was asked to take over as our district sales manager in the Hagerstown office. Ralph had attended Marshall College in West Virginia and had been quarterback for the football team there (which was a very important position). He had been a Nationwide agent for a couple of years before coming to Maryland.

I found Ralph a place to rent in Boonsboro, and he also attended Benevola Church. He and his wife Judy became very good friends with Ruth and me. Ralph and I not only went to church together; we played basketball together in my driveway. He could jump quicker and higher than anyone I had ever seen.

I had been writing a little over half a million dollars in insurance each year until Ralph came. He looked over what I had done the past years and then said, "Jim, I think you could sell a million." And the following year I did!

Now, anytime I won a trip for selling a certain amount of insurance, Ralph, as my district sales manager, won one too. So we sometimes traveled together. He and Judy and Ruth and I won a trip to Las Vegas once, and from there we went on to visit Judy's sister in California.

You Can't Outgive God

In 1971, Harry Newcomer made a special trip to our house to talk to us. He said he was purchasing some cemetery lots, and when we died he wanted us to be buried with him in those lots. I told him I considered that to be a great honor, but I didn't feel that we would be needing cemetery lots for a very long time. It was just one of the many ways he let us know how very special we were to him.

Soon after that, Ruth made a very troubling discovery: she felt a lump in her breast. She went to a doctor, and he tested her and found that the lump was cancerous. He recommended that the breast be removed. After the surgery, doctors told us that they felt sure the cancer had spread into the lymph nodes, which wasn't good.

Ruth received radiation treatments for a while (they didn't have chemotherapy available in this area at that time). At the end of her treatment, her doctors said they had gotten all the cancer and that she shouldn't have to worry. When all this happened, Ruth was so glad I had hired Doris to help with the responsibilities of the business.

Ruth had never been one to complain. One day, when I was out picking green beans, she came out and said she wanted to help. As she leaned over to pick beans, her breast form fell out onto the ground. That struck us both as funny, and we had a good laugh together. Ruth really enjoyed life.

There was a group of young women who got together for a meeting once a week, and Ruth loved taking part in that, but often now she didn't have much energy. She would go to the doctor, and he would give her a blood transfusion, and that would pep her up for a while.

Getting the transfusions, however, was a rather drawn-out procedure, with blood dripping into her one drop at a time. I remember one occasion when we had an engagement to play 500 after her transfusion, and we just barely made it in time.

Ruth adored her sons, Dale and Wayne, and she loved being a housewife. Many women of that time now wanted to work outside of the home, but Ruth once wrote a letter telling why she enjoyed being a housewife, which I thought was a bit unusual.

As noted earlier, Ruth had a beautiful singing voice and not only sang in our church choir, but also directed the junior choir and sang solos for weddings and other events.

In 1971 (and again in 1972), I was proud to have my picture in *Life Magazine*. It was with an article honoring the top Nationwide agents. The company prepared fliers with a picture of that issue on it, and we handed them out to our policyholders. In 1972, I won a trip to Puerto Rico, and Ruth and I and our two sons traveled there together. This was one of the last trips Ruth and I were to make together, and it was a rather strange trip. The people of Puerto Rico were expressing some anti-American sentiment at the time, and so we were told that we should not be out on the streets. One morning Ruth and the boys and I went down to the hotel restaurant and sat down to order breakfast, but, strangely, no one came to wait on us. Finally, I went to ask about it and was told that we would have to move to another table if we wanted to be served. They had no one to wait on the table where we were seated.

When we went on these trips, the usual procedure in the evenings was to have dinner, followed by a program. When we got there that evening, they had the program first, and it went on and on. Finally, they told us that they didn't know what was going to happen because the restaurant workers were on strike, so we just sat there for a while. Eventually, someone came in and said that the strike had ended, and we finally got to eat.

As Ruth began to realize that she might not make it, we had a frank talk about our lives — about whether there was anything that we would have liked to change. We both agreed that we didn't see anything wrong with our lives, just the way they were; we enjoyed what we were doing and saw nothing to change or improve on.

As Ruth's illness progressed, her doctor recommended a hysterectomy, and this surgery was performed. After the surgery, however, they couldn't get the bleeding stopped and had to give Ruth ninety pints of blood and platelets. She was in very good spirits that Sunday, and many people went to visit her. Her mother hadn't been to see her yet in the hospital, so I contacted her and told her she had better go visit her daughter, if she wanted to see her alive. She did that.

While I was visiting with Ruth on Monday evening, she went into convulsions, which wasn't a pretty picture at all.

The next morning I went to the hospital to spend the day with Ruth, and my good friend Ralph May came and spent the day with us. This really meant a lot to me then, and it still does. Ruth passed away that day.

Our son, Dale, needed a way home from college in Oberlin, Ohio, and Ralph went out and picked him up and brought him home.

When Mr. Newcomer had spoken to me a few years earlier about cemetery plots, I hadn't thought I would need them for a very long time. Now I needed cemetery plots and was pleased that I was able to purchase them not far from where he was buried. He had passed away in February of 1974, and Ruth died in May of that same year. She had lived just three years after having the mastectomy.

Ruth was very well liked and had many friends because she enjoyed life and mixed well with people. She wasn't a person who demanded or desired a lot; she was satisfied and happy with what we had.

More than nine hundred people attended her viewing and our family received about five hundred sympathy cards. Her funeral was held at 2 P.M. on May 20, 1974, at Benevola United Methodist Church. Our minister, Rev. David Stum, and our friend, Rev. Charles Lightner, did the funeral service, which was also very well attended. We had requested "no flowers," but she still got a lot. In place of flowers, we established a fund to buy a piano for the church in her memory, and more than a hundred people donated a total of $2,800 toward it (which was a lot of money in those days). That piano, a beautiful baby grand, is still being used by the church thirty-nine years later.

The church held a special memorial service in Ruth's honor, to dedicate the piano. Our eldest son, Dale, who was then a student at Oberlin Conservatory of Music in Cleveland, Ohio, planned the musical part of the program and played several beautiful selections on the new piano, and our youngest son, Wayne, who was then a senior at Boonsboro High School, made the formal presentation of the piano. To go with the new piano, Ruth's Boonsboro High School Graduating Class of 1948 donated a piano bench. It was an inspiring and meaningful service and a fitting tribute to a very special lady.

CHAPTER ELEVEN

DIFFICULT DAYS

When we lose someone we love, it is as if a part of us dies and is buried with them. When Ruth passed away, I could only sleep about four hours a night for the best part of a year, and I lost a lot of weight. I thought that year would never pass. I went through everything in the house to see what was there, and I gave away all of Ruth's jewelry and clothing to family and friends. Just before her death, I had purchased a farm. Let me tell you about it:

I've already told you about Mr. Harry Newcomer, who was the Register of Wills for Washington County, Maryland, and who was also our dear friend and relative and Ruth's employer. Around 1970 I started looking for a farm to buy. My good friend, Buzzy Everline, had purchased four acres of land from Mr. Newcomer's farm to build a house. When I learned of this, I thought Mr. Newcomer might be interested in selling the remainder of the farm. I placed a call to their home and spoke with Mrs. Newcomer. When I asked about purchasing the farm, she informed me that Mr. Newcomer was planning to give it to his nephew.

At the time, I didn't realize what an important phone call that was or how it would later impact my life. Without that phone call, Mr. Newcomer would never have known that I was interested in purchasing the farm.

Then, one day in late 1973, Mrs. Newcomer called me and said, "Jim, we're going to sell the farm, and you have first shot at it. If you don't buy it, another man, who is a member of our church, has asked to buy it. He's next in line. If neither of you wants it, we're going to put it on the market." I was both shocked and happy to hear this news. I had been searching for a farm to buy for the last three years, and the Newcomer farm was only about a mile from my house. So I went up to see Mr. Newcomer, and he asked me what I intended to do with the farm if I bought it. Even though I knew there was almost a mile of road frontage, which made the farm valuable and desirable for developers, I told him I was going to keep it as a farm.

His answer was, "If you were going to develop it or something like that, I wouldn't have sold it to you. But if that's what you are going to do with it, I'll let you have the farm." We agreed on a price that day, and I bought the farm – 160 acres, which included a stream of water and a nice house and buildings, for $85,000.

One day I said to Mr. Newcomer, "I guess we ought to write a contract for the farm."

He said, "Jim, we've been friends for all these years, and so I don't think it's necessary." I never thought anymore about it.

Then, in January of 1974, Mrs. Newcomer sent me a letter, which I still have, stating that they were selling me the farm for $85,000 at six per cent interest. Both of them had signed it.

However, in February, before we closed on the farm, Mr. Newcomer unexpectedly passed away. I thought it was rather strange that in that short period of three months, he was gone. After his death, I called Mrs. Newcomer and asked about the farm. She said, "Harry wanted you to have the farm, and so it's yours."

Mr. Newcomer's nephew and I had been the best of friends. Our wedding anniversaries were on the same day, and we always went out with them and another couple to celebrate. Now, however, he was upset because Mr. Newcomer had sold me the farm, and everything broke loose. We lost both couples as friends. Even people in our church took sides and thought it had been wrong of me to buy the farm. Some suggested that I had gone to Mr. Newcomer when he was old and vulnerable and had taken advantage of him, but my conscience was clear. I knew this wasn't true, and I didn't lose any sleep over it.

We closed on the farm in March, and Ruth died in May, so there was a lot of upheaval and hurt going on, even as Ruth was dying. My younger son Wayne was a teenager at the time, and he still remembers how all of this upset him and how our minister spoke from the pulpit concerning the resulting friction in the church. Wayne was hurt because he had lost his mother, and now he saw his father being mistreated and misunderstood.

For my part, even though I knew I had done nothing wrong, the pain caused by the way I was now being treated in this situation on top of the pain I was suffering from losing Ruth became a heavy load to bear.

Ruth passed away in May, so it was a good time of year to work on the farm, and that took my mind off of what was going on in my life. There was a large barn on the property that was eighty feet long, forty feet wide and forty feet high at one end. The barn needed painting, so I scraped all the loose paint off the whole barn and used a roller with a sixteen-foot extension handle to paint the whole barn. It took seventy-five gallons of paint, and it was a big job, but it was very therapeutic work for me. In the years that followed, I painted that barn two more times before eventually covering it with siding. Working on the farm and playing golf became my hobbies.

One field on the farm had branches growing close to the ground, with long thorns on them. One of us had to take a fork and lift up the branches, while another crawled in with a saw and cut them off close to the ground. There were hundreds of them in that field. After they were cut, we loaded them on a wagon and took them somewhere to burn them. My brother-in-law, Ellsworth Reeder, was renting the farm, and he and his son, Nelson, and Rick Toms, who was my friend Lehman Toms' son, helped me with this.

One evening, shortly after Ruth passed away, I was watching Billy Graham on television. Something came over me, while I was sitting there, and I couldn't believe how peaceful things got — just for a short while. I thought, "Surely this is the Spirit of God!" I have never felt that peaceful before or since.

After Ruth died, Dale went back to college, and Wayne continued his senior year in high school. We had a good neighbor, Doris Hoffman, who came in three afternoons a week to take phone calls and cook meals. Doris Baker, my secretary, lived right next door. I don't remember whose idea it was, but I had a business phone put in her house so that she could answer the phone when I wasn't there. She was a trooper, and it was kind of her to do that.

Being alone now, I had plenty of time to sell insurance, and I continued to make President's Club, even the year Ruth passed away. I also continued to win trips, but I now wouldn't go on them because I didn't want to go alone. One of the trips was a cruise, but I said, "No, I can't do that." I was dealing with two major losses in my life: the loss of my dear friend, Mr. Newcomer, in February, and the loss of my wife Ruth, in May. In my heart, I was hoping there would be better times ahead. I received a letter from our pastor's wife, Bonnie Stum, which was a great encouragement to me. Here's what she had to say:

You Can't Outgive God

Dear Jim,

We're on our way home from Canada. We're in Montana, headed for Glacier National Park, to camp tonight. It's been fantastic countryside, with the Rocky Mountains larger than we'd ever imagined.

I've been thinking a lot about you lately, with my increased leisure time, and thought I'd put some of my feelings down on paper. I still have not really comprehended the fact that dear Ruth will not be in our presence physically, and yet I feel her closeness so often. She gave so much to others and was always ready with a hug. Thanks for sharing her with us. It would have been easy for a husband to have been possessive with a wife like Ruth, but, thank God, you weren't. You helped to make her free enough to be open and share and love.

I regret that there were times of conflict and mis-understanding with us, but know that it's helped us all to grow and feel and know that God is with us and works through us (even in the bad times.) I cherish my memories of Ruth, as I know you do, every day. Forgive us when we forget you and get so involved in our daily routine that we misplace our priorities. None of us can feel your loss and, as a result, probably seem very inadequate in our efforts to reach out to you.

I'll probably sound like a parent, but I feel the need to say this: You're so young, and a whole variety of experiences are waiting for you. Don't hold back or feel guilty or worry about what others will think. It's your life. I did sound like a parent, didn't I? See you soon!

Love, Bonnie

Those words of comfort gave me more hope for better days ahead.

CHAPTER TWELVE

BETTER DAYS AHEAD

Many years ago, another agent told me that your business can get so big that even though you are working hard, you can't seem to make any progress. You think you're running, but actually you're standing still, and you can't grow anymore. The reason is that you're trying to do everything yourself, and there are only so many hours in a day. I remembered what he said and decided that it was time to get someone to help me sell insurance.

Rick Toms (who I mentioned in the previous chapter), had recently gotten out of college. He was working with a man who sold life insurance, but that company had not gotten him a license. So I said to Rick one day, "Why don't you come work for me and sell all kinds of policies. We'll get you a license and everything you need." The result was that Rick came to work for me as a sub-agent, and Nationwide gave him the schooling he needed to pass his tests and get his license to sell insurance. Rick had a nice personality, and he also knew how to work on a farm, so that helped me too.

At first, Rick was having trouble finding prospects. I said to him, "Rick, you've always got to keep your wheels turning, if you want to find prospects." I had no idea where that statement came from. I had never said it before. Of course, as Rick worked with me, he soon learned how to get the needed prospects, and he did a good job selling insurance.

One day, in the early autumn, I received a call from a lady named Ann who had lost her husband in April of that year. I remembered that Ruth had sent a card to her when her husband died. Ann called because she was in need of health insurance, and one of my current policyholders had recommended me.

I went to see Ann, and she explained what she needed. Nationwide had a good program for health insurance through the Maryland Farm Bureau. Anyone could buy the insurance, as long as they were a member of the bureau, so Ann became a member and bought the insurance.

Before I left Ann's house that day, I said to her, "It looks like we're in the same boat, having both lost our spouses. Would you like to have dinner with me?" She accepted and we drove over to a restaurant below Frederick for dinner. We dated for almost a year, and then, in July of 1975, we got married.

As I look back, it is amazing to me how, on two different occasions, someone said, "Call Jim Shifler." Those two phone calls drastically changed the course of my life. The first resulted in the call from Mr. Brady, asking me to get the captains for the United Fund in the villages in the southern part of Washington County. Without that phone call, I would never have met Mr. Brady and would never have become an insurance agent. The second call led to my marriage to Ann and our more than thirty-eight years of life together.

We had a small wedding. We invited Ann's son Lee and my two sons, Dale and Wayne, and our good friends, Eric and Kaye Lampard. Ann preferred to keep the wedding small, and it was followed by a reception at her home.

I liked working from my office at home and wanted to continue doing that, so I asked Ann to come live in my house. Her son came too, and the three boys slept in the same bedroom (since Dale and Wayne were both home from college). Ann was a good mother to her son and to my children as well. The better days I had hoped for had come, but they would require some adjustments.

CHAPTER THIRTEEN

ADJUSTMENTS

Ann is English. She was born in India, where her father was stationed in the military, but then she was raised in England. Some people couldn't understand why I would marry *a foreigner* and even asked if my new wife could speak English.

Ann had been a full-time actress back in England. She had attended school to learn acting and then made her living doing it. Some people at our church had a problem with my marriage to Ann, and, consequently, they weren't very friendly to her. I found that to be very sad.

I was still feeling the effects of the incident with the Newcomer Farm, so Ann and I decided we needed to look for another church. We ended up at Boonsboro Lutheran Church, where we attended and served for the next twenty years. The church required anyone who had served for three years in the same office to take time off, so I was president of the council three different times, for a total of nine years. When I wasn't serving on the council, I was doing other jobs in the church. Still, I had been a Methodist for so many years that I never considered myself to be a Lutheran and was never totally comfortable in that church.

Unfortunately, some members of our family also had difficulty accepting my marriage to Ann. This was hard for her, as you can imagine. She has had some rough roads to travel. I'm thankful that the passing of time has brought healing to these situations.

My marriage to Ann did not change my love for farming, and in 1975 or 1976, I was looking for a nice ten-acre lot to buy, but I couldn't seem to find anything I liked. Then I learned that the farm on Route 40-A, where my family had tenant farmed years before, was up for sale. I bought it. The owner had previously sold fifty acres off the frontage, so I got all the land in the rear of the place and all of the buildings.

When I got the farm, it needed a lot of repairs. A physicist had owned it last, and he and his wife were getting a divorce. There was work that needed to be done in every room of the house. The master bedroom had no drywall, just plastic hung up around the room. Rick Toms and Doris' husband Danny Baker both helped me repair the buildings.

I was blessed to have a family with three boys that wanted to rent the house, and they agreed to paint it inside and out. They lived in the house as my tenants for the next eighteen years, and you could go into the house at any time, and it would be as neat as a pin, even though they had three children. Tenants like that are hard to find.

Since this farm was next to my brother Charles' land, he asked me to sell him some land so he could raise steers, and I did that.

Adjustments

The barn needed some serious repairs. Termites had eaten the big wooden beam that ran through it, so it needed to be replaced. I removed all the partitions, so there were no longer stalls or places to feed animals, just one big, open space. There was a man who wanted to rent the barn, and he agreed to put the new beam in for me in exchange for a year's free rent. I also rented the land, so I had three tenants — one each for the house, the barn and the land.

The land along both sides of the lane, which was part of the 50 acres that had been sold, had been divided into building lots. I bought the two lots along the lane, made them smaller, and put a stipulation in the deeds that no shrubbery could be planted within 50 feet of the lane. Planting shrubbery in that area would have blocked the view from the farm house. After making the lots smaller, I put the rest back into farm land. The man who lives in the farm house now is so grateful that I put in the stipulation against planting shrubbery near the lane. The houses that were built on the lots sit back from the lane, and there is no shrubbery to block the beautiful view.

I would also like to share something about the people who rented the house on the Newcomer farm from me in 1978. I had never liked renting out houses, because it was so difficult to find good tenants. The personalities of the renters can make it either a pleasant or an extremely unpleasant experience. In trying to find good tenants for the farm house, I put an ad in the local newspaper, asking those who were interested in renting it to write a letter to me stating why I should rent the house to them. Howard and Patty Trenton wrote a letter saying that they would appreciate renting the house because they had a five-year-old daughter and a three-year-old son, and they wanted their children to have the experience of playing in the area around the house and seeing all the farm animals. They said they would take good care of the house.

This letter appealed to Ann and me, so we rented the house to the Trenton family. They lived there for eighteen years, taking good care of the house, but when they got ready to move, it needed to be painted. One day Howard stopped by to see me and tell me they would be moving into another house with his mother. He said, "Jim, don't worry; I'm going to paint all the rooms in the house, and it will be just like it was when we moved in." This really impressed me and made me very happy, because I didn't particularly want to do all that painting myself, and I thought it was hard to believe that someone would do that.

Now every year at Christmastime Ann and I get a Christmas card from Howard and Patty, with a note saying how much they appreciated living in the house. At Christmas 2011, this is what they said: "May your holidays be filled with love and happiness and the New Year bring good health. Memories of our farm house are always in our hearts. God bless. Love, Howard and Patty and Family."

We also got a Christmas card from their daughter, who is now grown.

CHAPTER FOURTEEN

OFF TO ENGLAND

After Ann and I got married, we traveled to England for three weeks at a time. We flew across the Atlantic to England, and then we took a train to where Ann's mother Doris and her second husband Jeff lived. Ann's father had passed away, and Doris had remarried. It was a very long trip. When Doris and Jeff picked us up, it had been about eighteen hours from the time we left home.

Cheriton Fitz Paigne is the name of the village where they lived. The village has a small school that is about a thousand years old and has a thatched roof, but is still in use today. There is a little post office, and someone had set up a table in a hallway inside the post office, where they were selling goat's milk. The village also has a pub and a small Methodist Church (that cost only a couple of thousand pounds a year to operate). They didn't have a minister, just lay ministers.

The roads leading to and from the village were so narrow that cars could not pass. One of them had to back up into what they called a "lay about" so the other one could get by. They also had very high banks along these roads, created by wagons and cars running over the roads for several thousand years and wearing them down, causing the banks on each side to get higher and higher. The roads are paved now, and it is a nice place to take a walk, because you are so far down between the banks that the wind can't hit you.

Doris and Jeff were married when they were in their 70s, but Jeff liked to joke by telling people that they "had to get married." Every day, at noon, it would be time for him to open up the bar and have a drink. One year, while we were visiting, Jeff took us a thousand miles to see Wales, where Ann had stayed for a time during World War II. Along the way, we stopped to see churches and castles.

We also stopped to see Stonehenge. These huge rocks sit in the middle of nowhere, and no one is really sure how they got there. Visitors were allowed to climb around on the rocks, but to preserve them that is no longer allowed.

We stopped at a village, where there was a ship sitting in the water. The next morning, when we got up, the ship was sitting on dry ground. That's how far the tides go out over there. Our tides here in the U.S. go out several feet, but over there, when the tide is out, you can walk out about half a mile, so that is quite a difference.

We were staying at a bed and breakfast, and I asked a man what unusual things we might see in the area. He told me about a church built in the 11th or 12th century. Because there was no religious freedom, and churches were not allowed, the people built this church in a very deep hole to hide it. We saw that hole. It is about five hundred feet wide, and the church sits down in it. They still hold church services there on special occasions.

While we were traveling in the car, when 11 A.M. came, Jeff would stop, open up the trunk (which they call a "boot") and get a little heater out to heat water for his tea. He would stop wherever we happened to be at the moment and have tea and biscuits. At 3 o'clock in the afternoon, he would do the same thing again. It didn't matter where we were, Jeff would pull off the road for tea.

Jeff came to the U.S. once and said he would like to live here, but couldn't afford to come, because of health insurance. In England, they have socialized medicine, which means that the government is responsible for all health care costs. Jeff was very handy and would often help other people in the village. He had a daughter who was difficult to get along with, he said, so he had left his son-in-law £2,000 in his will. Anyone who could live with that woman, he said, deserved £2,000. Jeff didn't live very long after that, but Ann and I have many fond memories of spending time with him.

I have been to England about fifteen times now, so I have a lot of good memories from there. It was interesting to see the difference between living in England and living in the United States. One time, when we were staying at a bed and breakfast, I got into bed and felt something strange in the bed with me. When I checked, I found that it was a hot water bottle, placed there to warm the bed!

CHAPTER FIFTEEN

A NEW OFFICE AND NEW SUB-AGENTS

In 1979 I moved my office into the downstairs area of my home, which gave me much more room. Rick Toms and Danny Baker helped me with the remodeling. Clients had been walking up those twenty-three steps to get to the office for the past eighteen years, and I decided it was time for something new. I had a local artist paint a beautiful mural on the wall, and we put in barn-wood paneling with big beams in the ceiling. I got a lot of compliments on the new office and a nice write-up in the Hagerstown newspaper. The following is an excerpt from that article, which appeared in *The Daily Mail* on Saturday, February 13, 1982:

BENEVOLA HISTORY STRIKINGLY PRESERVED ON OFFICE WALL

"Benevola" suggests a flow of good wishes, and the thought fills a lovely office in the tiny town of that name.

The "town" is not much more than a crossroads on Alternate Route 40, the old National Pike, as it approaches Boonsboro, but the spot has its own unique touch of history. A precious cameo of its heritage has been singularly preserved in a striking wall mural in the office of a Benevola insurance man, James E. Shifler.

The beautiful painting was done by John Roll, an area artist, from a photo taken in the 1840s of the small settlement where the National Pike was crossed by a road that wound its way from the area of San Mar and Mapleville to Roxbury and Williamsport. Roll spent more than a hundred hours on his fascinating project, including research on architectural details of the early 19th century.

Shifler lives in a stone house beyond the crossroads, one which he bought in 1951. The classic old building is shown in the upper right corner of the wall mural, fronting right on the pike.

An old map indicates that Jim's grandfather, W. Shifler, owned the same building in 1875 and operated a busy general store within its sturdy stone walls. When Jim purchased the house, from the heirs of William Stine, the "Benevola Country Store" was still a part of the crossroads. But Jim's business was insurance, so merchandising was discontinued.

A New Office and New Sub-agents

1840s PHOTO OF BENEVOLA CROSSROADS

Shortly after Jim moved into the house, the late Washington County Register of Wills, Harry Newcomer, gave him a 1840s photo of Benevola Crossroads, once known as Newcomer Cross-roads. Jim framed the small picture and hung it in his insurance office.

For twenty years that office was on the second floor of the house. The ground floor appeared unusable, since it was twelve feet high, "filled with junk," and not connected with the second and third stories by a stairway.

It was in 1978 that a lovely idea struck Jim's wife, Ann, that something special could be done with the lower level. The Shiflers consulted Eleanor Lakin, Boonsboro architect, and Daniel Baker, a "jack-of-all-trades" neighbor, and a consuming, wonderful project began.

Lakin made suggestions for laying out an office, a stairway, a bedroom, and a furnace room. Baker and Shifler took it from there, coming up with ideas as they went. Junk was hauled out, the ceiling lowered, the floor raised, and plaster sandblasted from the original stone walls. Shifler added to the atmosphere by using old barn boards for wainscoting and trim, and by retaining ceiling beams.

> For more than one hundred years the building
> had housed the "Benevola Country Store." An
> old meat-cutting bench was retrieved from the
> accumulation, and converted to a typing stand
> for Jim's secretary, and to a handsome coffee table.

A picture of the wall mural, with my wife Ann and me standing in front of it, is on the following page. By then, Rick Toms had been with me for several years, and when we moved into the new office, our policy count had increased to 4,900.

Soon after that, Rick met someone who started talking to him about selling alarms, and he decided that it would be easier than selling insurance. He went into the alarm business and did very well. He has about twenty people working for him today. He is also very active in the community. I only see Rick once or twice a year, but every time he sees me, he says, "I've got those wheels turning." We have remained close friends all these years.

When Rick left me to sell alarms, I realized how nice it had been to have someone help me make sales and take care of my policyholders. I had a nice office now, with three desks, and a new computer that Nationwide had asked me to install. First, I checked with my sons, Dale and Wayne, to see if they were interested in joining me in the business. They both said they couldn't deal with all the people, and they weren't interested in insurance.

With Ann in front of the mural painted on my office wall.

Dale had been an excellent student in high school, graduating second in his class. He attended college for six years, receiving his Master's Degree in music from New England Conservatory in Boston, Massachusetts. He is an excellent musician. Dale sold art for a period of time and has also traveled all over the United States playing the organ. He is now living in Hagerstown and plays the organ every Sunday at a local church.

Wayne also did well in high school, graduating in the top third of his class, and attended George Washington University for a few years. Then he transferred to Northwestern University near Chicago. Wayne recently married a lady from Thailand, and they are living there in her home country. His dream has been to become a famous author, and he is currently writing a book.

Before Ruth passed away, she said to me, "Take care of my boys," and I have been careful to look out for them all these years, even though they have not always lived in the local area. But having them as part of the business was not to be.

There was a life insurance agent who worked around the Boonsboro area named George Messner. He was married to a school teacher, and they had no children. I approached George, and we agreed that he would come to work for me as a sub-agent and that Nationwide would give him the training necessary to get his insurance license. I was now 54 years old and starting to think about retirement. (I decided to retire at 60).

A New Office and New Sub-agents

I started checking with other family members, to see if any of them was interested in selling insurance. One of my nephews said he would think about it, but he decided, instead, to go back to school to get his doctoral degree. He now works for the government and travels all over the world.

George and I were doing well, and I decided to hire another part-time secretary. Her name was Patty Null. News must have gotten around that I was thinking of retirement because a man named Jim Meadows, who had worked for several other insurance companies and was already a licensed agent, came to see me and asked if I would give him a job selling. If Jim came to work for me as a sub-agent, after I retired, he could go to work for Nationwide and get fifty percent commission on all my renewals for the first two years. After those first two years, he would get the same commission I would have been getting.

Jim had been working for me for a while when he came in one morning and said that another company had offered him a sizable salary to come work with them. He asked me how much of the agency he would get when I retired. I told him I couldn't do anything about that; he should go to see the district sales manager. He did that, and they worked out a plan to give him sixty percent of the policies. George would get the remaining forty percent. Jim did a good job selling insurance and also took care of my commercial accounts.

One evening Ann and I were playing 500 with a group of our friends, and Ruth's nephew and his wife were there. As I was talking with his wife, she told me they had a daughter in high school who was looking for a part-time job. So I called the young lady, Jennifer Cline (now Poffenberger), and she told me about her skills. I hired her, and she proved to be a very good secretary. Jennifer and I have remained friends all these years.

Later, when I started having the Sunday Brunch for the American Cancer Society, Jennifer always tried to sell a table of ten for me. She did this for many years. Jennifer is still very active in the community and raises money for various charities. I try to be generous and help her along in her pursuits. Right now she is in charge of a project to build a new scoreboard for Boonsboro High School, my old *alma mater*.

About a year and a half before I was to retire, Jim Meadows told me he would like to buy my home and insurance office and asked me how much I wanted for it. I gave him a figure, and a few months later he bought the home and office. Ann and I decided to build a new home on the Newcomer farm. My good friend, Buzzy Everline, who had purchased land from Mr. Newcomer, said "Why not build a home right beside us?" I told him we had decided to build on the other end of the farm, where there is a beautiful view of the valley and also of the mountains. From the spot we had selected, you could see for at least ten miles. Over the years, we have gotten much enjoyment from looking out our window at the scenery, especially when it snows in the wintertime. The snow on the trees and the mountains is breathtaking. The view is even lovelier when it's foggy. Observing the trees coming out of the mist is a sight to behold.

We hired a contractor by the hour to build the house, but he let me do any part of the building I wanted to. I put in the drainage around the base of the house, did all the painting and staining, put in the insulation, and, with the help of my niece's husband, did most of the electrical wiring. I also did all the landscaping, which involved planting about a hundred pieces of shrubbery. I was still selling insurance in my spare time, but I let my staff take care of servicing the policies.

Ann, being from England, wanted an English Wall Garden, and we put that in for her. So we now have a lovely home in the country. This past year two different people offered to buy this house, but it's not for sale.

CHAPTER SIXTEEN

JIM SHIFLER, MOTIVATIONAL SPEAKER

Ralph May was our district sales manager here in the Hagerstown area for about eight years, but then Nationwide asked him to go work in the home office in Columbus, Ohio. He accepted that position. One time Ann and I were out in Columbus, and we went out for Sunday brunch with Ralph and Judy. I was impressed with the waitress who served us that day. She said she enjoyed her job so much that it was like going to a party every day.

Later, Ralph became the regional sales manager for Arkansas and Mississippi. During that time, he and Judy lived in Memphis, Tennessee. He asked me to go with him to Little Rock, Arkansas, to speak to his agents. Ann and I drove a thousand miles to Memphis, and then I rode with Ralph to Little Rock, which was another hundred miles. When we crossed the Mississippi River into Arkansas, I was shocked to see all the rice fields. I had never heard about them, and now I was seeing them for myself.

While we were in the Memphis area, we visited Graceland, Elvis Presley's estate. I had never cared much for Elvis, but seeing Graceland was interesting.

On our way back, when we got to Knoxville, Tennessee, they were having the World's Fair there. Ann and I had been to one World's Fair in another area, not too long before that, so we weren't really interested in attending it again, but it was less than half a mile from the road we were traveling on, so we decided to go check it out. We got there about 2:30 in the afternoon.

As we were going through the gate into the fair, a man approached us and said, "Would you like to accompany us this evening for a nice free dinner? It will be at about 6 o'clock."

I said to Ann, "Well, I guess we'll be hungry by that time." So we went to the dinner. It turned out to be a time-share presentation. When the presentation was over, I said to the man at our table, "We're not interested."

He said, "You just sit right there." Then he went to the front of the room and made an announcement: "I want to congratulate Mr. and Mrs. Shifler for being the first ones to buy!" I was flabbergasted! So this was the way sales people conducted themselves. He was lying in order to encourage other people to buy. I was left speechless by his conduct, and we got out of there as fast as we could.

To change the subject for a moment, I won a trip, for selling insurance, to the Island of Maui, where a funny thing happened. We arrived at our hotel late in the evening, and

Jim Shifler, Motivational Speaker

Ann and I went to our room, which was on the 6th floor. Wanting to relax after the long trip, I stripped down to my skivvies and lay down on the bed. Imagine our surprise when a knock came at the balcony door. Ann went to the door and opened it, and in came a lady in a bikini. She and her husband were in the room next to ours, and they'd had an argument. She went out on the balcony, which was six floors up, and told him she was going to jump. Instead of jumping, she climbed across from their balcony to ours and came through our room to get to the hallway. When the other agents heard about this, I got a lot of kidding.

Now, back to my motivational speaking: Altogether I traveled to various places and spoke to various groups of agents about fifteen different times. I wonder what my friend, who thought I couldn't speak well, would have said if he had known that. In these sessions, I shared with the other agents the methods I had used to sell so much insurance. I was considered a pioneer in having a sub-agent work with me, and I would sometimes be asked to come and speak about how I made that work. Nationwide got the sub-agents licensed, but everything else was my responsibility.

Later on, Ralph May was regional sales manager in North Carolina, and they lived in Raleigh. It was the largest sales region and had more agents than any other Nationwide region— five hundred in North and South Carolina. Ralph asked me to go down to Myrtle Beach to give a talk. There were two or three of us giving speeches that day, and there were well more than a hundred other people in attendance at that meeting.

When Ralph finally retired, he and his wife came back to West Virginia. They had a very nice place there, and we went to visit them a couple of times. From time to time, he also came to see us and spent a few nights at our home. While he was here, he also visited with people he knew in the area. During his stay, we went golfing and did other things together.

About six years ago, Ralph was diagnosed with prostate cancer. He traveled to Tennessee to have surgery performed by a doctor who was tops in that field. He got along pretty well for a while, but later he started going downhill physically. He came to visit us, and we went for breakfast at Richardson's in Hagerstown. As we sat talking after breakfast, sharing about old times, Ralph turned to me and said something I will never forget. He said that out of the more than five hundred insurance agents he had worked with throughout the years, I was the best. That really meant a lot to me. I never dreamed he thought that much of me. As an agent, I knew I had to take care of three people: the company, the policyholder, and myself. If I thought the company was wrong, I would say so, and if I thought the policyholder was wrong, I would tell him. That always served me well.

When I started writing this book, I called Ralph's wife, Judy, to see if she would like to write something about Ralph to include in the book. She said it would be too painful for her to do that. I asked her to share something with me about Ralph. She said, "Ralph always said you were the best agent he knew and that you made everything look easy."

After talking with Judy, I thought a lot about what Ralph had said. Why had he thought I made things look easy? My grandmother used to say, "An idle mind is the devil's workshop," and I had firmly believed it. Each year Nationwide had a contest to see who could sell the most life insurance, and I always tried to get an early start on that. As I was reading the newspaper or talking with people, I was constantly looking for someone I could approach to purchase life insurance.

In horse racing, they say, "If you want to win, you have to be the first one out of the gate." I applied that principle to selling life insurance, and I never had to be concerned about trying to catch up.

My friend Ralph was very well liked, and when he passed away, another agent and I went to his memorial service, which was attended by about two hundred and fifty people. We had been friends for forty years, and I will always remember the things we did together, the good times we shared. It was a great friendship.

CHAPTER SEVENTEEN

HONORS AND AWARDS

In February, 1972, when I received Nationwide's magazine, *The Challenger*, I was surprised to see that there was an article on the front page with my photo. The article began as follows:

BOONSBORO AGENT IS TRAILBLAZER IN PRESIDENT'S CLUB – Makes Top Club 3 Ways

Like wilderness pioneer Daniel Boone, Agent Jim Shifler, 44, of Boonsboro, MD, proved himself a real trailblazer last year by becoming the first Nationwide sales rep to make President's Club three ways.

First, he multi-lined his way in, just as he did in each of the four previous years (1967 through 1970). Secondly, he P&D $1 million in life and met prescribed eligibility factors, to become a Life Millionaire's Award winner.

Finally, he won the life trophy as the life millionaire with the highest premium ($23,259 on a volume of $1,086,000).

You Can't Outgive God

It was a very interesting way to start an article. When I saw how many policies I had sold in 1971, the year the article referred to, even I was surprised. The article went on to share that I had sold 93 life policies (which shows that Mr. Brady did a good job teaching me how to prospect). It also said that I had sold 382 total policies, of all types of insurance, during that year and that I had built my agency to 3,370 policies in force. At that time, I had been selling insurance for eleven years, but had hired my part-time secretary just five years before the article was written, and, as you will remember, she only worked four hours a day.

I was pleased and honored that they had published this article in *The Challenger*. I was also pleased that they had included this: "Jim takes his church work very seriously and credits his success to 'the Lord being good to me.' " The article also noted that I was thankful to my first district manager, John Brady. It quoted me as saying, "He's the guy who recruited me and made it all possible."

Because of these accomplishments, the Nationwide agents from my own district also honored me by presenting me with a nice plaque.

In 1978, *The Insurance Salesman* magazine contacted Nationwide and asked for the name of one of their agents who sold a lot of casualty insurance and life insurance. Nationwide gave them my name, and they asked me to write an article. This came as a big surprise to me. How had I, who had never received a mark above a "C" in English on my report card, been chosen to write an article for a national magazine? As I wrote the article, I was thinking that nothing would ever happen with it. Imagine how shocked I was when they sent me a copy of the magazine with my article referenced on the cover as the "feature" article in that issue. Some of the other agents who had written articles had life insurance degrees, but my article had been chosen as the feature.

I hope my high school English teacher would have been happy with the article. Allow me to share it with you here. This is taken from the February 1979 edition of *The Insurance Salesman* magazine:

SELLING LIFE INSURANCE TO CASUALTY CLIENTS
"Ask a simple question....."
by James E. Shifler
Nationwide Insurance
Box 188, Boonsboro, Maryland 21713

Young people just graduating from high school and college provide a consistent, predictable market. And their parents will help you sell your program.

I have heard many multiple-line agents say that selling life insurance is too time consuming, and there are too many night calls. It's easier to find excuses why we can't do something than it is to find a positive way to accomplish the task. My time is valuable. I want to do a good job selling all lines of insurance and still have time to work on my farm and spend time with my family.

How do I sell a respectable number of life policies each year? After thinking it over, it seems there are four basic reasons — none of them new: (1) Know your product, (2) Believe in your product, (3) Recognize a prospect when you see one, and (4) Build the policyholder's confidence and trust in you as an agent.

Most agents will agree it is very important to know our product, but to really know our product takes continuous practice in the field. The agent who makes ten presentations a week will become a better salesman than the agent making only one. To be knowledgeable about the product requires keeping up with new ideas and sales methods, as well as the policy provisions. Still, many agents have difficulty doing this.

You know your product, but do you believe in it? There are many agents who sell life insurance but don't really believe in it. It is amazing how prospects and policyholders can tell if you believe in what you are selling. If you have to deliver a death claim, this will make you a believer. If you are a sensitive agent, and one of your policyholders dies without adequate life insurance, how do you feel? This should make you a believer, unfortunately, at someone else's expense.

Who should be approached to buy life insurance? My best market over the years has been young people who have graduated from high school or college and are getting their first jobs. I sell them anywhere from $5,000 to $25,000 of whole life, depending on their job and how their family handles finances. I make a point to find out the most convenient time to see them, when their parents can be present. Why? More often than not, parents sell the program for me. Checking the young person's finances and having parents present will help persistency. About 80% of the young people will use check-o-matic; this makes them start a checking account if they don't have one.

My company has a ledger book, which I carry for ages 21-45, for life insurance plans of $10,000, $100,000, and $250,000, both participating and non-participating. After selling a program, I order a ledger sheet and deliver it with each policy. The ledger sheet is a good tool years later, when the insured has a question about the policy, or when they want to add mortgage insurance, child rider,

or family rider to the base policy. The most important use of the ledger sheet, of course, is to show
the face value, cash values, paid up insurance, and
retirement benefits.

Many agents make life insurance too complicated.
People do not buy what they do not understand,
so we should make it as simple and as clear as
possible. That reminds me of a story:

An agent was trying to sell a pension case to a
group of employees. Before the plan could be put
into effect, all of the employees had to sign up for
it. All the employees did sign up, except Charlie.
The other employees and officers of the company
tried to get him to sign, but to no avail. Finally,
the foreman went to the company president and
said, "Look, everyone would like to have this
pension fund, but Charlie won't sign the paper.
Can you do something?"

The president went to Charlie and said, "Either
you sign this paper, or you're fired!" He signed
the paper immediately.

A few days later, one of the men asked Charlie
why he signed the paper for the president and not
for them. Charlie replied, "You never explained
it quite as clearly as he did."

How do I find my prospects? It's so simple that

it's almost embarrassing. When a policyholder phones or stops in my office about casualty insurance, after taking care of the problem, I switch to life insurance by simply asking key questions:

- Is your retirement enough?
- Have you bought mortgage insurance?
- Have you taken care of your inheritance taxes?
- Shouldn't your son or daughter be starting an insurance program of their own?

Many people will know right then whether or not they want some kind of a plan or program. All that remains to do then is to make a simple sales presentation. Three life sales last year came in this manner from a sixty-year-old father. He initially called me about his car insurance and also bought three whole life policies: a $20,000 rated policy on his seventeen-year-old son, $10,000 for his twenty-year-old daughter, and $20,000 on his twenty-two-year-old son. The father is paying half the $800 annual premium on the three policies. Because he initiated these policies, the children will appreciate them and continue to keep them in force. By asking simple questions to policyholders last year, I sold over $1.75 million on a hundred lives. I still had time with my family, took a month's vacation, and worked on my farm. There was time to do all this and still service more than 4,600 policies that I have in force.

It takes more than being educated, believing in your product, and knowing who is a good prospect. If you lose the trust and confidence of your property/casualty policyholders, you will have trouble selling life. And if you do sell them, you'll have trouble keeping the business on the books. Their trust and confidence in you as an agent will sell many life policies with little effort.

Several years ago I received a call from a mother who wanted her sixteen-year-old son who was working part-time to buy life insurance from me. She remarked that she did not quite trust another agent, who wanted to write a $15,000 whole life policy on him. The other agent had the first three requirements for the sale, but did not have the trust and confidence of the mother.

Over the years, I have given a great deal of thought to how to be fair to my policyholders, my company, and myself. What better way to take care of all three than by selling life insurance? It gives the policyholders the financial security they need; it is a profitable product for the company; it gives me easy sales and peace of mind, knowing my policyholders have complete insurance programs.

This article shares much about my philosophy of selling insurance, and I considered it a great honor to be chosen out of all the other agents to have the article featured on the cover of the magazine. If an agent gives good service, his policyholders will sell policies for him. This helped me a lot in building up my agency. Much of my business came to me through referrals from other policyholders.

As I shared earlier, when I first became a Nationwide agent, another agent told me not to sell insurance to farmers, because he didn't understand them. I had spent the first eighteen years of my life learning how to work on a farm, and I also owned two farms. Because of this, I was knowledgeable about the kinds of insurance that would benefit farmers. I sold them all kinds of policies — life insurance, health insurance, fire insurance, liability insurance, automobile insurance, and retirement insurance. As it turned out, about thirty percent of my business was to farmers. I understood their needs and could talk their language, so my beginnings on the farm were very important to my later success as an insurance agent.

In 1980, *The Challenger* published an article stating that I now had 4,900 policies. The headline in big letters was "MARYLAND PRO BUILDS ON TRADITION." Following are the first three paragraphs of that article:

Almost 150 years ago, his great-great-great-grandfather earned the respect of Boonsboro, Maryland, by operating a community grocery in a huge, graystone house along a major roadway. Today Nationwide Agent Jim Shifler, 52, of Baltimore Sales Region, commands the esteem of his peers in the still-rural Boonsboro area. And his agency and residence are headquartered in the same graystone house, now a landmark.

With approximately 4,900 policies in force, Jim and Nationwide have become synonymous with insurance there, particularly within the farming community.

At the end of each year, Nationwide would honor the agency that was number one in sales that year. We agents would get points for every policy we wrote. I was never near being number one on this, because it was necessary to have a very large agency to be at the top, and we were just a small country agency. Imagine my amazement when they called me in 1985 and told me I was third in the company out of 4,800 agents. I was very proud to receive this honor and pleased that I had sold 587 automobile policies, 177 fire policies, $62,500 in annuity premiums, $27,095 mutual fund reduction, $37,650 group and $159,522 in commercial premiums. We wrote $6.2 million in life insurance policies and were number two in the company on that score. We had a net gain of 1,032 policies that year, giving us a total of 5,505 policies.

Other agents often kidded me that I must have a lot of family members to sell that much insurance. I was proud to say that my brother Seibert was one of my biggest policyholders, and my two other brothers and my sister and her husband were also good policyholders. Not only did they buy insurance from me, but their children did too. Members of my first wife Ruth's family were also my policyholders. As noted earlier in the book, sometimes people say you shouldn't deal with family members, but that didn't hold true for me. Family members were some of my best clients. I was also glad when I could help some of them buy their first homes.

When I retired in 1987, I had more than 2000 policyholders, and they had purchased 6,300 policies from me. That year I had $3 million in premiums from these policies. If someone had told me that this would happen to me back in 1959, when I passed my first insurance test, I would never have believed them. It didn't seem possible for this to happen to someone like me, who was born and raised on a farm, graduated from high school with just a "C" average, and who had an office in such an inconvenient location, in the country with few homes nearby, and where people had to climb 23 steps to get inside. In addition to all that, I could never attend school to learn to be an insurance agent, because I was working for Potomac Edison forty hours a week, as a meter reader, and some people told me I would never make it as an insurance salesman, because I didn't talk well enough. Again, I must give God the glory for blessing me and giving me great favor with my clients. I enjoyed serving them and selling them insurance that would benefit and help them in their future.

When we made President's Club, we had to wait until the following year to go on our free trip. So, in 1988, after I retired, I won a trip to San Diego, California, as the dean of the President's Club. It was a large convention, with a big room full of people. The people who were new to the club and who had the least years were called forward first to receive their awards. In 1987, out of 4,800 agents, 148 of us made President's Club. I was proud that I had made President's Club for twenty-one consecutive years straight and had been dean for the last five years of my career. Since I was the dean, I was the last agent to be called forward, so I went out with a bang.

The year before I retired I got a surprise call from the home office. They said that Mr. Fisher, the president of Nationwide, was sending a company airplane to Hagerstown to pick Ann and me up and fly us out to Columbus, to the home office, so that we could be honored before the Board of Directors. They had a luncheon, where Mr. Fisher presented me with a silver platter for being in the President's Club for twenty years. They flew us back to Hagerstown on the plane later that same day. Our district sales manager in Hagerstown at the time, Dan Whaley, hired a limousine to take us to and from the airport. I will never forget the feeling of pride and accomplishment that I experienced that day and how good it felt to be appreciated for the years of hard work I had invested in my chosen career.

CHAPTER EIGHTEEN

"EVERGREEN"

After I retired from Nationwide, Ann and I enjoyed traveling to parts of the United States we had not previously visited. Our good friends, The Lampards, had joined a Bed and Breakfast Club called "Evergreen," and Ann and I decided to join too. We participated in this club for about ten years. After paying a small entrance fee, you could stay in the homes of other members for just $25 a night. When you joined, you provided them with information about your home and your hobbies. You could choose where you wanted to go and arrange to stay in the home of one of the other club members in that area. In return, other members of the club would call and make arrangements to stay in your home. This turned out to be a lot of fun, and over the years we had thirty-six different couples stay with us. Many of them came to our area to visit the Antietam Battlefield.

Since Ann and I enjoy playing Bridge, I usually tried to find a couple to visit who also played. Since a lot of the club members were Bridge players, we had the privilege of traveling to and playing Bridge in many parts of the

United States. We really enjoyed meeting so many nice people, and we stayed in some wonderful homes.

One time we made arrangements to stay with a couple in Florida. When we arrived there, Ann wasn't feeling very well. In fact, we had stopped at a medical center on the way, and they had prescribed some medication to help her. I asked our host where I could get the prescription filled, and he said he would take me to a drug store, but first he wanted to tell us that he and his wife were nudists. Thankfully, they kept their clothes on while we were there.

Once we were visiting some people in South Dakota, who had previously traveled to Paris, France, and they shared a humorous story with us that happened while they were there in Paris. They both had to use the rest room, but when they found one, they discovered that there was a fee to use it, and they had no money with them. There was an attendant there, so they tried to communicate with him that they didn't have any money, but he didn't respond. After trying unsuccessfully to get his attention, they assumed that he didn't understand English, so they decided to climb over the barrier and use the rest room anyway. Imagine their surprise when the attendant shouted, "Hey, you can't do that!"

There was a couple who lived in Alabama, who were listed as members of Evergreen, and Ann and I wanted to stay with them and visit some nearby flower gardens. When I called to make the arrangements, the lady of the house answered, "I don't know what you're talking about!" It turned out that her husband had joined the Bed and Breakfast Club and failed to tell her about it. I think he was retired, and she was still working. We got the confusion straightened out and went to stay with them, and he turned out to be a great host. He put fresh flowers in our bedroom, and one day when we went to the gardens, he paged us there and made several suggestions concerning what we might like to do next.

Another time we went out West to stay with a couple and play Bridge. They lived about a hundred miles from Mt. Hood, and we were able to see it clearly from their home. Another time we spent eleven days sightseeing out West and covered twenty-nine hundred miles.

One of the nicest trips we took was to Holland, Michigan, which is known for the Veldheer Tulip Gardens. In the month of May, when the tulips are in bloom, they hold a week-long festival, which includes a play, a parade, and many other events. The whole town participates in this, and the streets are bordered with brilliantly colored tulips.

Since we were in Michigan in May, we thought the weather might be chilly, but it was warm, sunny, and beautiful, and we had a truly delightful time (see the photo on the following page).

Ann and I have done a lot of traveling and have had the pleasure of visiting every state in the U.S., with the exception of Nebraska. I am very thankful that we had the opportunity to meet so many wonderful people and to see and enjoy so much of this magnificent country.

A tulip field at Veldheer Tulip Gardens in Holland, Michigan

CHAPTER NINETEEN

SECRETS OF SUCCESS

After I had been retired for several years, I started thinking about my career as an insurance agent, trying to analyze how I had been able to sell so much insurance. The first thought I had was that I had been only 32 years old and in the prime of life when I started selling insurance. I realized that the things I had learned growing up on the farm, attending school, serving in the Navy, and working for Potomac Edison had all been invaluable to my career in insurance. I also knew my friend and first district sales manager, Jack Brady, had taught me a lot that had contributed to my success. As I pondered all of this, I came up with a list of more than forty principles that I felt had been important to my being a successful agent.

When I was using these "secrets" to sell insurance, I never gave a thought to the fact that some of them, like my high energy, good health, and personality, were actually gifts from God. I just used them to get the job done and, at the time, I didn't give the Lord the credit that I should have. I trust that this book has rectified that oversight. I would like to share twenty of those principles with you here:

You Can't Outgive God

1. Believe in your product.
2. Be honest and conscientious.
3. Be a good listener.
4. Be a self-starter.
5. Learn to recognize a prospect when you see one.
6. Be willing to go the extra mile.
7. Have a pleasing personality.
8. Watch people's reaction. It can say more than words.
9. If you can help it, never pick up a piece of paper more than once.
10. Maintain good health and hygiene.
11. Always dress appropriately.
12. Be a soft salesman.
13. Like the company you work for.
14. Build people's confidence and trust in you as an agent.
15. Have a good office location.
16. Have the right people working for you.
17. Keep the wheels turning.
18. Have a lot of energy.
19. Have a hobby.
20. Keep it simple (kiss).

Instead of waiting for people to come to my office, I sold most of my life insurance to people in their homes, where they were more relaxed. When I had an appointment, I was always on time, and I tried to be cheerful, with that same smile I'd had as a young child. I was a very good listener and learned to watch the people's reactions to the things that were being said. By doing this, I could usually tell whether or not I was about to make a sale. I was a low-key talker and made my presentation in a very simple way.

I had prepared a ledger sheet, which I used to show my prospects how much life insurance I was trying to sell them, how much it would cost, the value each year, and how long they had to pay for it. I would also share whether it was permanent or term insurance and would explain that the sooner they bought it the less they would have to pay for it.

On the farm, I reminded them, we always tried to bring the grain in from the field as soon as possible, because a lot of damage could occur if a big storm came along. Or, someone could accidentally leave a gate open, and horses or cattle could get into the field and damage the grain. The longer we waited to harvest a field, the more risk we were taking. If we let the grain get too ripe, some of it would drop to the ground and be lost.

In much the same way, many people wait too long to buy life insurance. If a person waits until they are older, life insurance becomes more expensive, and many times the person is in poor health by then. This causes them to pay a higher premium or makes them ineligible to buy it at all. I explained to my prospective customers that by buying right then they would have peace of mind, and if something happened to the head of the household, the family would be provided for. Once the wife understood this, she would usually encourage her husband to buy the policy.

You Can't Outgive God

Parents helped me sell insurance to their children, many times paying the first premium themselves. A great time for me to sell insurance to a young person was when he got his first job. I was the only agent I knew of who sold a lot of insurance to young people, and I did very well with it.

I also did well selling to older people. Some people didn't believe in life insurance or didn't buy because no one had explained it to them. I always took the time to explain life insurance to them.

By doing the things I have outlined here, I sold about a hundred life insurance policies a year without having to resort to high-pressure sales tactics. By the time I retired, I had $33 million of life insurance on the books.

Many insurance agents preferred to sell to people who came in with a definite need, like car insurance, fire insurance, or business insurance. They were satisfied to sell these kinds of policies and didn't want to take the time to sell life insurance. But if I was going to be a person's insurance agent, then why not sell them life insurance, rather than them waiting for a salesman from a life insurance company to do it? That way they would have all their insurance at one place.

I always worked two evenings a week and tried to sell my life insurance at the first of the week. Then I could concentrate on other types of insurance the rest of the week. A lot of agents said, "When I have time, I'll get around to selling a life policy," but since they didn't have a time set aside to

224

do it, it never got done. We had twelve agents in the district, and I had more life insurance in force than all of the others combined.

Number 6 on my list is to be willing to go the extra mile. One time a fellow brought someone to my office wanting a donation to help start a ball team in Boonsboro. Without giving it much thought, I gave him $200. The man was amazed that I would do that, because he didn't even have insurance with me, and his real estate agent had only given him $15. My wheels weren't turning that day, or I would have taken the opportunity to check on his insurance needs. Sometime later, that same man called me. His lawyer said he had to get a buy-and-sell agreement, and he needed a $200,000 life insurance policy, so he decided to give me a shot at it. My quote was competitive, and he gave me the policy. I also wrote his homeowners', his vehicle insurance, and his business insurance, and I later sold his three children each a $50,000 life policy. Altogether, he probably spent $40,000 a year with me. This happened because I was generous and willing to go the extra mile.

A man came to my office who had just gotten out of prison and was in need of car insurance. Since he had been in prison, I couldn't put him with a regular company, so I sold him what they call an "assigned risk" or "substandard" policy. I never gave it much thought after that. Several years later, he called me and told me he had bought a company. He said, "You were nice to me, so I want to give you all my insurance." He had fifty men working for him, with a payroll of about $1 million. He gave me his workman's comp, his liability, his fire insurance, and I wrote life insurance and health insurance on all his employees, and life insurance on him. The year I retired, his premiums to Nationwide were $100,000, and all of this came about because I had been kind to him, remembering what I had learned in Sunday school.

Item No. 5 on my list is to recognize a prospect. A manager from Nationwide called and asked to go along with me to see someone who might be a prospect for a retirement policy. As we were driving down the road, I told him, "When I worked for Potomac Edison, I cut this fellow's lights off." That put some doubt in the manager's mind as to what kind of reception we would receive when we got to the place. When we arrived, the client was fine and even bought a retirement policy from me. The manager couldn't get over that: I had cut this fellow's lights off, and still he bought an account from me. What I didn't tell the manager until later was that I had known this man for many years, and we were good friends. In fact, we attended high school together for a while.

When I sold retirement accounts, we had an HR10, which was like an IRA. I bought an HR10 back in the 1960s, and after many years, it had greatly increased in value. When I found something that was doing well for *me*, I liked to sell it to others, so it could help them, too.

There was a man who had his four vehicles insured with me, so I thought he would be a good prospect for a retirement account. I went over the account with him and asked him how much money he could put in the account, and he gave me a figure. I told him I would have to see his income-tax return to see if he qualified to put that much in. When I looked at his income tax return, it showed zero income, which made him ineligible. To qualify for an HR10, he had to earn a certain amount of money, so sometimes a client wasn't a good prospect, even though he appeared to be one.

Another time I went out to see a certain farmer. He and his wife were both in their thirties, and they had recently been blessed with their first and only child. So I knew he should be a good prospect. I didn't make an appointment, but I knew when he milked his cows, so I went out to see him and caught him in the milking barn. He asked me what I wanted, and I said, "I thought you might be interested in a life insurance policy."

His answer was, "Well, I don't have any money."

If I had stopped there, I would have missed the sale, but when someone said "no," I always tried to say something low pressure to change his mind. I said, "Let's wait until you're finished milking, and we'll go in, and I'll tell you what I have and talk it over with you and your wife." He agreed to do that.

When he finished milking, we went inside, and I presented a program to them, which was a whole life policy, with some term insurance, that would pay a good sum of money if anything should happen to him. The premium would be about $400 a year. When I finished making my presentation, I said, "Don't you think this would be a good thing for your wife and family?"

"Yeah," he said, "it would." Then he turned to his wife and said, "Now, mother, go get the checkbook and write him out a check, and next year we'll put in some pigs to pay for it."

Number 19 above is to have a hobby. If a person is to work hard, they also have to have something they enjoy doing to relax. As noted earlier in the book, my hobbies have been farming and golfing. I enjoyed playing golf in the afternoons and am happy to tell you that I have had three holes in one.

Another related hobby of mine is looking for lost and abandoned golf balls and selling them to raise money for charity. Over the years, this hobby alone has enabled me to donate more than $25,000.

As for my hobby of doing manual work on my two farms. I never really considered it "work." I enjoyed it and found it relaxing. It took my mind off of selling insurance for a while.

The last item on my list is to keep it simple. I once saw the need for that in a fellow agent. Sometimes Mr. Brady would have me handle a situation, if he thought it might be received better coming from me than from him. There was an insurance adjuster who was giving that up and applying to be an agent with Nationwide. He was going out to see a man who wanted a tenant's homeowner's policy. He didn't have a house, but was living in an apartment, and wanted a homeowner's policy to cover his furniture. Mr. Brady asked me to go with him, so I did.

The agent gave this man a long spiel, talking and talking. The man had already said he wanted the policy, but the agent kept going on and on, almost driving me nuts. I found that agents many times oversold, when all that was necessary was to keep it simple and say something the person could understand and relate to.

They're simple, but these have been my secrets of success.

CHAPTER TWENTY

RETIRED, BUT NOT SLOWING DOWN

When I finally retired from Nationwide, Ann and I were very good friends with two other couples: Eric and Kaye Lampard and Phil and Penny Crabtree. We played cards and golf together and visited each other's homes. Phil was on the board for the American Cancer Society, and, before I retired, he had asked me if I would also serve on that board. I told him to wait until I retired. So when I retired in December of 1987, I remembered my promise, and I attended the first meeting of the local board in March of that next year. I found this worthy cause to be the place where I could use the extra time and energy afforded me by my retirement. Since my first wife, Ruth, had passed away as a result of breast cancer, this cause already had a place in my heart.

Dr. Harold Gist was president of the board, and I was greatly impressed with his leadership and his devotion to the American Cancer Society. He became a wonderful friend and role model to me. Soon after I joined the board, he asked me to be in charge of fundraising, and I became involved with their two main fundraisers: selling daffodils each spring, and the "Longest Day of Golf." A local golf course would let the golfers play as many holes as they wanted in a day, each golfer would find sponsors who would pay so much a hole, and all the proceeds were donated to the American Cancer Society. My team and I played 54 holes of golf in one day, and some people played even more than that.

Later Dr. Gist asked me to be the president of the local Cancer Society and still continue as chairman of fundraising. When Ruth was living and our sons were younger, we normally went out for Sunday brunch. In 1989, I got the idea of having a Sunday brunch as a fundraiser for the Cancer Society. I talked it over with Dr. Gist, and he told me it would never work, but he was willing to give it a try. I contacted Frank Turner, who owned the Ramada Convention Center, and he gave me a price for a nice Sunday brunch. We charged $15 a ticket, and that first year, without sponsors, raffles, or silent auctions, we raised $5,000. This brunch became an annual event for the next twenty-one years, and the last year it was held, 2010, we raised more than $34,000.

Looking back, it almost seems like a fairy tale. How was it possible? The success of the brunches was achieved by the continuing dedication of many people. Once the brunch was established, Lou Scally (a local TV celebrity) served as the Master of Ceremonies and "Dean Burkett and Friends" produced balloon sculptures and did magic tricks, while Mary Jane Koontz provided face painting. In addition to the generous contribution of these individuals, the brunches could not have succeeded without the sponsorship of more than a hundred merchants who purchased ads in a booklet we put together. We also started a silent auction.

People wondered how I accomplished so much, but I never felt pressured. I would start working on the brunch in the middle of August, and the event was held on the first Sunday in November. I went out to see about a hundred business owners, to sell them ads, which I really enjoyed. If I had just sent the requests out, instead of going to see them, I wouldn't have gotten nearly as many ads. I gave each merchant an addressed envelope and a copy of their previous ad. They made any changes they wanted in the ad, put a check in the envelope, and dropped it in the mail. When they saw me coming, a lot of people would just say, "How much do I owe you this year?" It was enjoyable raising money for such a worthy cause.

When I started the Sunday Brunch, Rick Toms suggested that when someone sold a table of ten we should give them a discounted price on each of those tickets. This worked out well over the years. The final year of the brunch, more than twenty people sold tables of ten for me. With their help, I sold over five hundred tickets. My great friend, Dr. Gist, continued to attend the brunch throughout his life, even coming in a wheelchair, after he'd had his legs amputated.

People loved attending the Sunday Brunch because it afforded them an opportunity to socialize with friends they may not have seen since attending the brunch the previous year.

Of course, none of this would have been possible without the help of all those who sold tickets. One of those people was Grace Snively, who is now 99 years old. Grace worked with me for many years on the Daffodil Days project and the Sunday Brunch. When I phoned her one year and asked how she was doing, she said, "Not so well."

I said, "Then, Grace, you probably don't want to help me this year."

Imagine my surprise when she said, "Jim, I will help you to the day I die. Send me ten brunch tickets and twenty-five raffle tickets." Would you believe that she sold twelve brunch tickets that year?

In 1992 I received an exciting phone call from the home office of Nationwide, announcing that I was one of eight agents out of forty-eight hundred who were being inducted as a charter member into their newly-formed Hall of Fame.

In 1992, I was interviewed for an article in *The Daily Mail*, the Hagerstown newspaper, by reporter Bill Callen. The following is a copy of that article, which appeared in the "Just Folks" column of the paper on August 21, 1992:

RETIRED, BUT NOT SLOWING DOWN

Honored Insurance Salesman Now Hustling for Cancer Society

Boonsboro — Jim Shifler tells a story of meeting a fellow retired insurance salesman in England a couple years back. The man, Shifler says, declared that his working days were done, that never again would he bust his hump after a lifetime of evenings and weekends on the job.

Shifler's glance sweeps the rolling fields that, in the distance, fold into a town nestled this morning in a fuzzy blanket of lazy haze. It's an elegant, blissful view, the kind to be enjoyed with a cup of black coffee and a James Michener novel, where time need be marked only by the advancing sun and the shifting, bracing breeze.

It's a view that seems to say, "Congratulations, you've earned it. Take a break." But Shifler's thinking about enclosing the deck. Unlike the man in England, he's got work to do.

"I just think you should be active in your community," says Shifler, bearing down on 65. That's why he agreed four years ago to become the chief fundraiser for the Washington County chapter of the American Cancer Society, an organization that raised more than $97,000 last year for cancer research and education.

Since he came on board, the local chapter has climbed from near the bottom to the middle of the pack statewide in per capita donations, raising an average of 83 cents per person last year, 17 cents more than the average person gave in the bordering counties, Frederick and Allegany. Shifler is generous with his praise for others in the organization, especially its former chairman, Dr. Harold Gist. But it's difficult to underestimate the influence of a man so adept at sales that he recently was named one of eight charter members of the Nationwide Insurance Hall of Fame.

Shifler sold insurance for Nationwide for twenty-eight years, starting as a part-time agent, and retiring four and a half years ago with more than 2,300 policyholders covered by $33 million in life insurance alone. For twenty-one of those years, he was in the President's Club, which recognizes agents who are in the top 3% in sales in the company.

Before becoming an insurance agent, a move encouraged by Nationwide's district sales manager, after Shifler organized a United Way fund drive in South County in the 1950s, Shifler spent eleven and a half years with Potomac Edison, where he fixed lines, delivered and repaired appliances, read meters, and, every fourth week, took his turn collecting bills on weekends.

Each of his ventures have built on the other, Shifler says. Potomac Edison taught him customer service. Insurance sales taught him that to ask others for their money, he had to believe in his product.

"Whatever you're doing, you've got to believe in it," says Shifler, tanned and fit and dressed for a round of golf, which he plays with a 15 handicap. "At least it's that way for me."

Shifler's first wife, Ruth, died of cancer eighteen years ago. He remarried a year later, to a widow who came to him for insurance after her husband died. "I sold her the insurance," he says with a smile, "and ended up paying the premiums." Ann Shifler is a long-time volunteer with the hospice program in Washington County.

A couple of years before he retired, Shifler says, a policyholder who was on the cancer society board approached him about volunteering. Shifler asked him to wait. He wanted to do the job right, and didn't think he could as long as he was running his business. When he retired, he remembered.

An associate once told him he'd never be a salesman, Jim Shifler recalls. He said he was too laid back.

A hundred and sixty acres of farmland spread before him. A big home, where even the pea gravel in the driveway is tidy, is on the other side of the sliding screen door. Laid back, indeed.

I thought it was an excellent article, and I always appreciated, not only that I was able to give to my community, but that they also gave so much to me in return.

I came up with something that I could do to raise money for charity. (I mentioned it briefly in the previous chapter.) I was amazed at the way some golfers didn't spend much time looking for their lost balls. When I grew up on the farm, we were taught never to be wasteful, so I started collecting abandoned golf balls at Beaver Creek Country Club, where I was a member. I would put a dozen golf balls in a plastic bag, sell them for $7.00 and give the money to charity. I sold the balls to individuals, but I also contacted three local businesses that agreed to sell them for me. Any balls I was unable to sell in this way were purchased by Family Recreation Park near Hagerstown; over the years, they have purchased many thousands of golf balls from me. Mr. Jack Barr gave me their ball striper, and I have striped all their golf balls for years.

Sometimes people give me golf balls they are no longer using. I get as many as a thousand golf balls a year this way. Altogether I have been able to donate more than $25,000 to charity from the sale of these golf balls, and, as I mentioned earlier, this has become an enjoyable part of my hobby of playing golf.

In 1995 the National American Cancer Society was trying to start what they called a Relay for Life in Washington County. The organization suggested that we send out a letter to the public and offer them a free meal if they would volunteer for the project. The lady who was director of the Hagerstown division talked to our board, but they didn't seem interested. As president, I just let them talk. Then, when they had already said they weren't interested, I said, "We're always *looking* for people to help us raise money, and it's not costing us anything, so why don't we try it?" And, with this, the members of the board agreed to give it a try. I could see that the director was impressed that I had been able to get the board members to change their minds, and Relay for Life became our top fundraiser. In 1995, we also had seven hundred people attend the Sunday Brunch, raising $14,800, so it was a very good year of fundraising for the cancer society.

I didn't really give this much more thought until the following year, 1996, when I learned that I had been selected as Volunteer of the Year by the Maryland State Division of the American Cancer Society. There was a nice article in *The Daily Mail*, the local Hagerstown newspaper, announcing my selection. Before receiving that honor, I wasn't even aware that such an award existed. Apparently, after I had successfully changed the minds of the local board members about the Relay for Life, the director of the Hagerstown division had written to the state division, sharing all the data she had collected about my work with the Longest Day of Golf, Daffodil Days, and the Sunday Brunch. Others said it was a much-deserved honor, but I always found the work enjoyable and was glad I could serve such a worthy cause.

Soon after that, I heard that Benevola United Methodist Church was planning a major project. They wanted to enlarge their parking lot and construct a new addition to the church. When I heard about it, I felt that it was time for me to return to my roots, where my heart was, so I went back and again became a part of that church. The people there seemed happy that I had come back home.

I have enjoyed being back at Benevola United Methodist. It took Ann a little longer, but she didn't like going to the Lutheran church by herself and finally joined me at Benevola.

Enlarging the parking lot was no problem, but when the church officers put the new addition out for bids, they were surprised to learn that it was going to cost over $1 million. They took a vote from the congregation, and it passed, so they decided to move forward with the project.

They asked me to be on the Building Committee and also to be chairman of the Outreach Committee, where I served for a number of years. I was pleased to be a part of planning the new construction.

I never thought a small church like that would be able to pay off such a large sum, but Benevola Church is very active, and we were able to pay for the entire project in about six years. The congregation has grown, and the church is now able not only to meet all of its own obligations, but also to give more to help others outside the church.

CHAPTER TWENTY-ONE

GOD'S HEALING MERCY

I shared earlier in the book how God brought me through a near-fatal illness as a child. After that, I enjoyed excellent health, until about the age of 65, when I had to have my gall bladder removed. About that time, Johns Hopkins Hospital asked Ann and me to join a research program they were doing in four different locations around the United States. Hagerstown was one of those locations, and people in this area were being asked to participate, so we volunteered.

For the first several years, they gave us a complete physical each year, and then, in later years, they called us on the phone and asked us questions about our health. In January of 2012, they again did a physical examination, one that took ten hours.

During those early years, as they were doing the physical exams, if they found something that they didn't like, they would give us a paper to present to our local doctor so that he could follow up on it. This happened with my good cholesterol, which was 26, but they said it should be 40. My local doctors didn't think this was anything to be concerned about. They gave me my regular check-ups and also stress tests, and everything seemed to be fine.

For a number of years, Ann and I had gone on vacations to Myrtle Beach with our good friends, the Lampards and the Crabtrees. Then, while we were there one year, I did a little workout in the morning, and a short while later I suffered the worst pain in my chest that I have ever experienced. I drove to the hospital, which was about four miles away, but when we got there, Ann went to park the car and I walked into the Emergency Room. It was a small, satellite hospital in South Myrtle Beach, and there was no waiting. They put me on an examination table right away.

By now, I knew that something was very wrong, and I remember thinking to myself, "Good luck, Ann! If something happens to me, you will have two farms and a house to take care of or get rid of." Soon after Ann arrived at my room, my heart suddenly stopped. The doctors quickly got her out of the room and began working to restart my heart. When they called her back in, they explained to her that they were going to give me a medication that they hoped would save my life, but that it could cause me to bleed or possibly could even kill me. I bled a great deal, and some of the blood went into my bladder, which was extremely painful.

Tests showed that my aorta valve, which has been nicknamed "the widow maker," was about ninety percent blocked. I was transferred by ambulance to the main hospital in Myrtle Beach. After I was admitted, they put me in my room and told me I had to lie still for twenty-four hours. This was difficult because the blood in my bladder was making me very uncomfortable. The next day they inserted a stent to open my aorta valve. Three or four days later I was discharged from the hospital.

Ann had to drive us back to Boonsboro, which took thirteen hours, since she has never been a fast driver. At first, I sat up front with her, but the pain was so great that I thought I would never make it home. When we got to Interstate 95, Ann stopped for coffee, and I decided to get into the backseat and lie down, and that made things a lot better. When we got as far as Brunswick, Maryland (only about twenty miles from home), Ann wanted to stop for lunch, but I pleaded with her. "Ann," I said, "I'll be glad to take you out to lunch, but not today." So we drove straight home.

My good friend and neighbor, Buzz Everline, arranged to take me to my local doctor's office. Doctors in Hagerstown suggested that I undergo physical therapy to regain my strength, but I asked them if I could walk instead. They agreed that walking would be as good as physical therapy, so I went out my front door each day, and I've been walking ever since. I have missed very few days, and if the weather is bad, or it's too cold, I go over to our church and walk around the basketball court.

They continued to check my heart several times each year. At one point they said the heart wasn't as strong as before, and they sent me to Baltimore to have a pacemaker and defibrillator installed. That was about five years ago. Doctors are able to check these apparatuses by telephone every other month. They do it while I'm fast asleep.

Later, I again experienced pain in my chest, and they sent me to Baltimore, where they put in two more stents. I learned that you are supposed to have at least seventy to seventy-five percent blockage before doctors resort to inserting a stent, and one of my arteries had been only fifty percent closed. It seemed that they had done it just to make money, so they could bill my insurance, and so this was reported to my local doctor. He suggested that I file suit. If I got anything from it, I could give the money away to charity, but I never heard any more from it.

I am amazed at what I am still able to do. I play golf, work in my garden, and I continue to help others in any way possible. I am very thankful to God for sparing my life. If I had passed away, Ann would have been left with the farms to sell, and she knew nothing about the tax issues. Because I lived, I was able to sell the farms myself, and we did well for ourselves and were also able to contribute a lot to charity. This would never have been done if I had died that day, so it may be the reason God kept me here.

CHAPTER TWENTY-TWO

MORE ADVENTURES IN ENGLAND

Ann and her sister Audrey decided to buy a house in a small town in England called Witheridge. Their mother's second husband, Jeff, had passed away, and Audrey had lost both her husband and son. Audrey and Ann wanted to bring their mother to live in that house.

Many of the houses in England are very small. The house they bought had just two bedrooms, a living room, and a kitchen, as well as an attached garage. Altogether it was about 650 square feet. Most of the appliances were miniature (compared to our appliances here in America). The property had a very nice flower garden and a small front yard.

Each year Ann went to England for three weeks. I usually went every second year, and while I was there I tried to do something that needed to be done, like painting the house. I was amazed at how different things like tools, paint, and paint brushes are in the UK. While I was there, I also helped some of the older ladies in the village with odd jobs. I got to know a farmer who lived in the village, and he helped me several times. Audrey was surprised at how many people I got to know in that little village of about a thousand people.

There were three churches in Witheridge, but the attendance in all three combined was less than one hundred. I attended church once in the winter, and the church was so cold that the ushers wore overcoats, when they collected the offering. I was glad to learn that this church later installed a heating system.

The people in Witheridge walked a lot, and they didn't seem to mind the rain and the cold weather. Near the village, there was a farm with a right of way through it that was several miles long. The farmer was required to provide a way for people to walk from one field to the next without climbing any fences. While I was there, I also took walks. There were different length paths, and you could select the one that was the distance you wanted to walk. You went straight through the farm, and when you came to the fence there was either a gate or something a person could walk through but a cow could not get through. The farmer was allowed to do this in any way he chose, as long as people didn't have to climb the fence. I really enjoyed walking down the roads and across the fields.

The taxes are very high in England, including a "value added tax." Some have been suggesting that we use this same system here in the United States, but it is a very bad tax. In England, everything is taxed seventeen percent, even repairs. Gasoline, or "petrol," as they call it, is very expensive. One time we rented a car there, and the gas tank was nearly empty when we got it. Before I returned the car, I tried to get the gas in the tank down to that same level. Audrey said, "Jim, you ought to get some gas."

I said, "Audrey, it was almost empty when I got it, and so we're going to keep driving."

As noted, one of my hobbies is golf, and I played at two different courses while I was in England. Some things there seemed very strange to me, and I thought other golfers would enjoy hearing about them.

First of all, there are no golf carts. Sometimes you even see men walking their dogs while they are playing golf (which wouldn't be allowed here in the U.S.).

Over here, you can't play golf while there is frost on the green because it will kill the grass. On their golf courses, they have a little area of green beside the fairway with a circle around it, to use for a putting green early in the morning when the frost is still on the ground. They don't care if you kill that grass.

Another thing that seemed strange to me was that they don't want you to wear blue jeans to play golf. Often the English golfers roll their pants legs up to avoid getting them wet, which I thought was rather funny.

I played golf with one man there for a number of years, until he moved away. Once, hearing that I was there in the village, he came back, called me up, and we went golfing. At lunchtime, we went into the club, and I offered to buy his lunch. He ordered first, and then I ordered. The waitress asked me what I wanted to drink, and I told her "water." Her immediate response was, "Where in the hell did you come from?" Most people in England are tea drinkers or, if not, must have their alcoholic beverage. A lot of English people, including Ann's mother, couldn't get over the fact that I drank water all the time.

Another man took me golfing at the oldest golf course in England. It's called the Royal North Devan Golf Club, and it was started in 1864. The club actually owns only one hole of the course — the 18th hole. The rest is owned by the surrounding farmers, and there are horses and sheep on the course. They place red ribbons around each hole to keep the animals away. On the score card, with the list of rules and regulations, they state that if your ball lands in manure, you are allowed to move it.

This course is located by the sea, and when we teed off, we had to hit the ball over the seaweed, or there might be seaweed right in the middle of the fairway. One hole was a par 4, which is usually about 400 yards long. Once in a while, someone can hit a ball that far, but it is rare. Usually it takes two shots. This par 4 has a sand trap in the middle of the fairway, about 160 or 170 yards out. Behind the sand trap, there is a board fence, ten or twelve feet high, so if you hit a shot, and it isn't straight enough or high enough, you can hit that board fence. One time, when I teed off, something very unusual happened that you would never guess. My shot wasn't high enough, and when it hit the board fence, the ball got stuck in a knot hole in the fence and stayed there. The odds are definitely against that ever happening to anyone again. My many fond memories of playing golf in England include playing on the course with the horses and sheep and getting my golf ball stuck in the fence. Also, the no jeans rule, playing in the frost, and people walking their dogs on the course.

About five years ago. Ann's sister Audrey was diagnosed with cancer and became very ill. Ann had been communicating with her each week by phone, but now she felt she needed to go to England to see for herself how Audrey was doing. The same day Ann arrived, Audrey became so sick that they had to call the doctor in the middle of the night, and they both spent the rest of the night at the hospital. Ann called me the next day and said she would like me to come to England and help her, which I did.

To get to the hospital, we had to take a bus from the little village of Witheridge to a larger town, about an hour's drive away. When we got near the hospital, instead of dropping us off at the last stop, the driver always took us the rest of the way to the hospital. We were surprised and grateful that he would do that. It may have been because we were strangers. Since we were from another country, we were not allowed to drive Audrey's car, unless we got written permission from her insurance company and paid a special fee.

You Can't Outgive God

Bus transportation in the UK is free to those who have reached a certain age, but even though we were old enough to qualify, we had to pay, since we were not citizens of the UK.

Audrey had no plans in effect concerning who would care for her in case of a serious illness, so Ann and I had to come up with a plan. Audrey had no children, but she did have two nieces and two nephews. Of the four, we decided, her niece Karen would be the best one to care for her, even though she lived about a hundred miles away. We talked our plan over with Audrey and then called Karen to see if she would agree to it. Karen and her husband graciously agreed.

When Audrey thought she was well enough to go home, she left the hospital, but after just a few days at home she realized it wasn't going to work. She reluctantly came to the conclusion that she would have to give up her home. I called Karen, and she and her husband found a very nice nursing home close to where they were living that would take Audrey. And they got in touch with someone in the government and were able to get free transportation to move Audrey to the home.

After that, I had to contact a lawyer to change Audrey's will and another lawyer to draw up a power of attorney for Karen. I also had to sell Audrey's house, car, and motor bike. I called a real estate agent who wanted a one and a half percent commission to sell the house. I asked him if he could do it for one percent, and he agreed. Due to the exchange rate, he would be earning more than what one percent would be here in the United States. The British pound was worth about $1.50 in U.S. currency at the time. They were getting ready to transfer Audrey back to the hospital that day and the real estate agent got there just in time to get her signature on the contract. The two attorneys went to the hospital to get her signature on the will and power of attorney.

I was amazed that I was able to take care of all those legal matters in a foreign country. Audrey died about six months later. Ann had to go back to England twice, once for the memorial service and again when Audrey's ashes were interred. Audrey was a lovely lady, and we enjoyed spending time with her, both in England and when she came to visit us in our home here in the United States. She is the aunt I referred to who had passed away just before Gary came to see us in the introduction of the book.

I wanted to share another story about Gary. This one happened just before he went to China. He and his wife and two sons were visiting with us. The boys were about seven and nine years old at the time. Gary's wife wasn't feeling well, so I agreed to entertain the boys. I gave the younger one a golf club, and he went out behind the house and hit golf balls. Gary and his older son went golfing with me. Later that day, I took the boys bowling and then out to eat at a Chinese Restaurant.

I also took the kids to visit the Antietam Battlefield. In the visitor's center there, they show a very nice movie about

Abraham Lincoln and the Civil War that I thought the boys would enjoy. The one boy went to the movie with me, but the other one went into the gift shop to see what was there. After the movie, they both looked around the gift shop for something to buy. One wanted this and the other wanted that. I told them, "You're going to be traveling to China," so I wanted to get them something they both could enjoy. This didn't seem to please them. After a while, they came to me and said, "We had a meeting, and we decided that would be okay." I thought it was funny for young boys to say they'd "had a meeting."

The final day they were to be with us, I wanted to take them to visit Washington, D.C., which they had never seen before. So I said to the kids, "I'll take you to Washington." The boys said they were going to have a meeting.

After their "meeting," they said, "Instead of going to Washington, we want to go golfing, bowling, and to the Chinese Restaurant." I was surprised that they wanted to go back and do the same things we had already done.

I had a good time with the boys, but we never did get to Washington, D.C. The next day Gary and his wife and children left for China, to begin their service as missionaries.

CHAPTER TWENTY-THREE

IT'S A BLESSING TO GIVE

After my retirement, Ann and I took many vacations to Florida. Once, while we were there, I received a phone call from Ed Wade, the pastor of Victory Baptist Church back home. His church was interested in purchasing a piece of land on Route 40-A in order to build a new church building, but they had a problem. The people who had sub-divided the land into lots had put a stipulation in the deed that it could not be sold for any commercial purpose. Since I owned the land adjacent to the property the church wanted to buy, Pastor Wade asked me to sign a paper that would give them permission to build their church on this land. I knew they couldn't build a church there unless I signed off on it, so I agreed to meet with him and do what was needed. The following is a letter I received from Pastor Ed Wade, thanking me for helping their church:

Dear Bro. Shifler,

This is a letter of appreciation to Jim Shifler for the help he has given Victory Baptist Church over the years!

When the land upon which the church now resides was being purchased, we had to get approval from adjoining land owners, because of zoning regulations. Jim graciously granted his approval. Years later, as the church grew and an expansion was needed, again Jim gave us help. He donated a parcel of ground connected to the rear of our property so our building expansion could move forward.

A few years after that act, when Jim was in the process of selling his farm property, which lies behind us, he generously donated two full acres to our church. This land is now used for youth activities and a sports field.

Jim has a giving heart and God has used him to assist many organizations through his material giving, as well as his efforts in raising other funds. God Bless you, Jim, and thanks so much for your kindness to Victory Baptist Church.

"Lay not up for yourselves treasures on earth ..., but

lay up for yourselves treasures in heaven…"

The letter was signed, "Sincerely, Edward J. Wade, Pastor."

I believe that when we have a desire to give, God opens up opportunities for us to bless others. When I drive past Victory Baptist Church, I experience a warm feeling of satisfaction. I thank God that He gave me this opportunity and the financial means to aid this congregation in spreading the Gospel.

CHAPTER TWENTY-FOUR

GIFTS AND OPEN DOORS

Over the years I asked several different ministers whether or not I was called by God to be an insurance agent. They all told me, "No, you don't have a calling." But I kept on wondering how someone with my background could become such a successful insurance agent. Then I found a scripture in the Bible that spoke to me about the gifts that God puts in each one of us. It is found in Romans 12:4-8:

> *Just as each of us has one body with many members, and these members do not all have the same function, so in Christ we who are many form one body, and each member belongs to all the others. We have different gifts, according to the grace given us. If a man's gift is prophesying, let him use it in proportion to his faith. If it is serving, let him serve; if it is teaching, let him teach; if it is encouraging, let him encourage; if it is contributing to the needs of others, let him give generously; if it is leadership, let him govern diligently; if it is showing mercy, let him do it cheerfully.*

You Can't Outgive God

When I took my personality test, I was able to see more clearly the gifts I had been given. I only wish I had known it much sooner. I now understand that these gifts were given to me by God, and I have had them since birth. The personality test showed that I was an extrovert, which means that I like and am good with people. That ties in with serving, encouraging, and giving in the above scripture passage. I truly enjoyed serving my clients and saw them as my friends. When they had a problem, I would do my best to encourage them and help them with that problem. This kind of service built their confidence and trust in me as an agent. As a result, my policyholders sent many other people to me for their insurance needs.

As I have shared with you already, giving generously has been a way of life for me since 1956, when our pastor, Curvin Thompson, preached about the farmer who tithed his potatoes. When we give, God promises to bless us financially. Luke 6:38 says it like this: *"Give and it will be given to you. A good measure, pressed down, shaken together and running over, will be poured into your lap. For with the measure you use, it will be measured to you."* In Malachi, the last book of the Old Testament, God asks us to put Him to the test concerning tithes. He promises to *"throw open the floodgates of heaven and pour out so much blessing that you will not have room enough for it."* I can assure you that God keeps His promises. My life is the proof. I would never have dreamed that I would have such a successful career as an insurance agent. I also did well when I sold my two farms. I know that everything I have or ever will have is a result of putting God's teachings about giving into practice in my daily life. It just goes to show that you really can't out-give God.

On that personality test, I also scored high in sensing, thinking, and judging, which means that I like to base my decisions on logic and to do things in a planned, orderly fashion. You could see this in the fact that I never had a lot of papers on my desk. In fact, due to having five people employed and only three desks, I was often working on the coffee table. I was taught not to pick up a piece of paper more than once and also to solve problems as soon as possible, rather than letting things fester. These traits tie in with the leadership gift in Romans 12:8.

I also shared earlier that my personality was much like my Grandfather Easterday and my mother, Ellen Shifler, who were both positive role models for me. They were cheerful, likeable, hard-working individuals that other people enjoyed being around. I consider it a gift from God and a blessing that I am like them, and I know that this has been a tremendous asset to me throughout life. I just naturally like to reach out to people and get to know them. James 1:17 tells us: *"Every good and perfect gift is from above, coming down from the Father of the heavenly lights, who does not change like shifting shadows."*

I also believe God opens doors for us, and our success or failure depends on whether or not we enter those doors.

You Can't Outgive God

That is one of the reasons I wanted to write this book. I want other people to think about the opportunities God has opened up for them and to encourage them to take the steps of faith necessary to enter those doors. If I had failed to do that, my life would have been very different, and the money I have been able to give away would never have come to me, and the people I have been able to help would not have received that help.

Let's take a look back at the open doors I have experienced and the times that God has intervened and directed my life. First of all, God placed me in a Christian family on a farm. There I not only learned about the Lord and was involved in church, but I learned how to treat others and help them, and I learned how to put in an honest day of hard work. All of my brothers and my sister have also done well because they were hard workers, too.

As a young child, I survived a deadly disease, spinal meningitis, receiving a healing from God, when the doctor had said I could possibly die. Then, about ten years ago, God spared my life again, when I suffered that near-fatal heart attack. My heart actually stopped, but they were able to get it restarted, and I am still alive and active these many years later.

God gave me a positive outlook on life, and I was known as always having a smile on my face. He also made me a very energetic person, which enabled me to work long hours, both on the farm and, later, as a meter reader and insurance agent. When I went to work at Potomac Edison, the first thing most of the other workers did in the morning was go for a coffee break. I didn't drink coffee, so often I went out and started reading meters ahead of them.

My release from the Navy two months early was definitely an open door for me that started a whole chain of events in my life. Without the intervention of God in arranging that early release, I would never have gotten the job with Potomac Edison.

Since I knew so many people from reading meters all over the southern part of Washington County, I was prepared for the next open door. Mr. Brady came to see me and said someone had suggested that I would be a good person to find chairmen for the United Fund in each of the small villages in the southern part of Washington County. He was so impressed with the way I did that job that he offered me a job with Nationwide.

I chose to keep my job with Potomac Edison and work for Nationwide part-time at first, and I took over a small insurance agency. Because of the gifts and the personality God had given me, I did well selling insurance, and the vice-president of the tri-state region for Nationwide came to see me and encouraged me to take a full-time job with the company. That was a big decision for me, and it was another door I had to walk through to find the success God had waiting for me.

As an insurance agent, I always worked two evenings a week. Neither my first wife, Ruth, nor my second wife,

Ann, ever complained about me working those two evenings. When I wasn't home, they both also took countless
telephone calls for me over the course of the twenty-seven
years I was selling insurance. My job wasn't a nine-to-five
one, like a lot of others, and having their help has been a
great blessing and was, therefore, instrumental in my success.

I also consider the people God sent to work with me to be
a special gift. Doris Baker and my other part-time secretaries, Patty Null and Jennifer Cline, and my three sub-agents,
Rick Toms, George Messner, and Jim Meadows, helped everything fall into place, as we built a very successful agency.

Nationwide was a great insurance company to work for,
and they showed much appreciation to me, as an agent.
They were also a company that was interested in the family.
When I was with Nationwide, they opened a lot of their
meetings with prayer.

My great friend and district sales manager, Jack Brady,
looked out for me almost like a father looks out for his
own son.

For my part, I was always ready to make money, but I
was also interested in selling the policies that were right for
the policyholder and would best meet their needs. Helping
people in this way was very rewarding and fulfilling for me. I
know that God opened these doors. I took the steps of faith
to walk through them, and so I ended up exactly where I
belonged and where I would have the best opportunity to
serve others and, in doing that, to serve my God.

Gifts and Open Doors

I have received many awards and honors in my life. It is amazing to me that I had the opportunity and privilege of working for Nationwide Insurance, one of the top hundred companies in the United States. It is even more amazing that my name and my face are on an engraved plaque hanging in the Nationwide Hall of Fame in the twenty-five-story Nationwide Insurance Building in Columbus, Ohio. I was greatly surprised and blessed when the president of Nationwide sent the company airplane to Hagerstown to pick Ann and me up and take us to Columbus to be honored before the Board of Directors.

Reading this book and learning about all the things I have seen and done may make you think that I am some kind of outstanding or special person, but, you see, I know something about me that I want to be sure you understand. I am just Jim Shifler, a simple, ordinary man, who serves an awesome, wonderful, extraordinary God.

CHAPTER TWENTY-FIVE

THE SHIFLER FAMILY COMMUNITY CENTER

One year, just before Christmas, I was in downtown Hagerstown and there observed the actions of a Salvation Army worker. It was a very cold day, and this lady was standing outside in the cold, ringing a bell and encouraging shoppers to place donations into a Salvation Army kettle. I was very impressed and thought to myself, "What dedication, to do that!" From that time on, I began sending a check to the Salvation Army each year around Christmastime.

A good many years later, I had occasion to go to the Salvation Army office for something. (At this point, I don't even remember why I went there.) What I do remember is that when I got there I spoke with a man named Harry Barger (who is still with them to this day). It must have been in the spring of the year, because that's when the Salvation Army holds their annual Appreciation Dinner. Harry invited me to attend the dinner, and I did. I discovered that the Salvation Army is a wonderful group of devoted and dedicated people who have the call of God to serve Him and to serve the people of our community. Soon after that, I was asked to serve on their Board of Directors, which I have done for the past fourteen years, taking an active part and serving on several different committees.

After I had worked with the Salvation Army for a few years, they asked me to become Chairman of the Board. I declined because I was still working with the American Cancer Society. It took about two and a half months each year to prepare for the Sunday Brunch. Besides the brunch, I had the rest of my work with the Cancer Society and was serving in my own church, so it didn't leave me much free time.

The price of farm land had been increasing steadily, and in 2003 I felt it was probably about at its peak and decided it was time to sell part of the farm with the stone house on Route 40-A. I had in mind to sell about ten acres of land and the house and buildings. As it happened, farm prices actually rose a little more the following year, and one man said to me, "You sold it too soon," but I got nearly top dollar for the farm.

The first couple who came to look at the farm was Mr. and Mrs. Steve Brightwell. They wanted to purchase twenty-five acres and the house and buildings, and they made me an offer. I thought I could probably get more than they offered for it, but they were such a nice couple, and I could see they would make a good addition to the community. I decided to let them have the farm. Just as I thought, they turned out

The Barn on the Newcomer Farm

to be super-nice people and did a lot of work to improve the house, putting in new wiring and plumbing and finishing off the attic into bedrooms and an office.

My wife, Ann, had a grown son who had to have some minor surgery. What a shock it was to all of us when he failed to recover from this minor surgery and passed away. I said to Ann, "Lee was such a nice person, and now he will never inherit any of our money. Why don't we give a gift in his memory to the Boonsboro Library?" We gave one-third of the proceeds from the farm sale to the Boonsboro Library in memory of Lee Miles, Ann's son, and they put a nice plaque in the library in his memory. I put the rest of the money from the farm into a retirement program for myself.

I already shared with you about the nice farm I had purchased from Mr. Newcomer. It was only a mile away from where I lived. I did several different projects to improve the farm, including putting metal siding on the house and barn and all new windows in the house. One year, a bad tornado came through the farm, causing a total of $100,000 worth of damage to five buildings. I replaced two of them with a new pole barn, to house the hay and machinery. The barn on this farm, which is pictured on the previous page, is one of the nicest ones that I know of in all of Washington County.

At one point, I decided to put the land on this farm into the land preservation program. This actually devalued the farm, because it could no longer be developed. Someone asked me why I did that. I told him that I had promised

Mr. Newcomer before I bought the farm that I would keep it in farm land. The guy said, "You didn't have to do that. Mr. Newcomer is dead!"

My answer to him was, "I promised Mr. Newcomer." So, regardless of whether he is living or dead, a promise is a promise, and I am a man of my word.

Three years ago, four different people approached me to buy the Newcomer Farm. One of these was my tenant farmer and his wife, Mr. and Mrs. Brian Baker, and his accountant, Gary Holtz. I consulted with my real estate agent, and we arrived at a selling price, so I didn't have to pay a real estate agent to sell the farm. A long time before this, my accountant had told me that I should give my two sons some shares in the Newcomer Farm, and I had done that. So when I sold the farm to the Bakers and Gary Holtz, my sons got paid for their shares. I kept a fourth of the proceeds.

While considering what to do with the rest of the money, the thought came to me that I should give part of it to the Salvation Army. This was something I had never thought about before.

The people at the Salvation Army were extremely grateful for the gift, which was $300,000, and they explained that they had been wanting to build a multi-purpose building for forty years. My contribution was the sparkplug that would now get them going. They already had $100,000 in their treasury from previous donations. They asked me if I thought I might consider giving another $300,000, and they would name the building after me. I reviewed my finances. I knew I could sell the remaining thirty-seven acres of the farm on Route 40-A, and I still had a building lot I could sell. If I could do that, it seemed, I would be able to contribute the second $300,000 without touching any of my savings. I agreed to their request.

I objected, however, to the building being named after me. "That isn't necessary," I said, but no one seemed to be listening. They insisted that I have this honor.

I was also made Honorary Chairman of the fundraising campaign and my photo was put in the fundraising packet. They asked about fifty of us to go out and visit prospective donors, to raise more money for the building project. I personally visited more than a hundred people and was able to raise well over $100,000 in additional funds. I even had three people call me on the phone, and each of them gave $10,000.

Now the Salvation Army of Hagerstown had nearly enough money to build their new building, and so they broke ground and got started early in 2012. I sold the thirty-seven acres to Matt Murphy for a horse farm (He now has fifteen horses), I was also able to sell the building lot, so my financial plan for giving the additional money worked out well.

They asked me to decide what to name the building. I wanted to include other members of my family, because my first wife, Ruth, and my present wife, Ann, both helped me

The Shifler Family Community Center in Hagerstown, MD

a lot over the years, and their contributions were vital in making it possible for me to give this money to the Salvation Army. In the end, we decided to call it the "Shifler Family Community Center." The ribbon-cutting and dedication of the new building was held on Sunday, October 14, 2012, at 3 P.M. It was dedicated as follows: "We dedicate this building to the character building of youth, the fellowship of believers, as a house of prayer, and to the preaching of the Gospel in word and in deed, to God be the glory!"

During the dedication ceremony, Lieutenant Colonel Jack Waters from the Salvation Army came and sat beside me and expressed how grateful they were for my contribution to the building. He said that since I was able to provide most of the money up front, it had also saved them thousands of dollars in interest. The new building houses a beautiful gymnasium, a computer center, with ten computers, and offices for the ministry staff.

The building that was previously used for the offices is now being converted into a dormitory for battered women and children. The Hagerstown Salvation Army was previously able to provide housing for twenty women, and this project will double their ability to serve in this vital ministry.

The new gymnasium will be used as a gathering place for the young people of our community — a safe place where they can learn how to live good, clean lives, build strong character, and be given the opportunity to come to know Jesus as their personal Savior. I was pleased.

The Shifler Family Community Center

Mr. Newcomer's surprising decision to sell me his farm now became a real blessing to me and to others. I owned the Newcomer Farm for thirty-four years. Over the years I sold off various parts of the land, and when I figured it up I discovered that the overall amount I received for the farm represents an increase of fifteen times what I had originally paid for it. By doing further calculations, I discovered that my increase on the other farm, the one with the stone house on Route 40-A, was ten times what I had originally paid for it. In addition to this, I had received an income from the farms for more than thirty years. God certainly blessed me with an over-abundant increase! In the last eight years, I have given away more than $1 million to three charitable organizations. In addition to this, I have tithed for fifty-seven years, most of the time giving more than ten percent, so I really have no idea of the total amount I have given away.

I recently received a call from World Vision thanking me for having supported them since 1980. I started out by supporting one child, and, more recently, began to support two. I would never have dreamed that I would be able to do all these things.

When I was young, my goal in life was just to have a family and a house. I didn't consider ever having a lot of money. Even when I had the two farms, I never thought about them being worth a lot of money in the future. I just enjoyed having them and working on them. It didn't enter my mind, until I was ready to sell them, that they were worth so much money. God has truly given a remarkable increase!

As noted earlier, the Bible tells us (in Malachi 3:10) that if we tithe, God will open the floodgates of heaven and pour out so much blessing that we won't have room enough for it. When I started tithing in 1956, I had no idea that this would happen to me, but I can say that God has been true to His promise. He has blessed me more abundantly than I could have ever imagined, and simply because I did what I learned in a sermon at church. I certainly never thought that anyone would name a building after me.

Looking back over my life, it seems too good to be true. God has spared my life on two occasions, protected me from situations that could have destroyed my future, guided me in investing money and making decisions, even when I wasn't aware of His guidance, and used this poor farm boy who couldn't even afford a basketball. I well remember how I used a soccer ball, a half-bushel basket for a hoop, and a barnyard for a court, when I was learning to play the game. Again, I also remember the thrill I experienced when I was a freshman at Boonsboro High School and had my first opportunity to play basketball in the gymnasium. Now I have been able to help provide a beautiful new building with a gymnasium where other young boys and girls will be able to play basketball while being shaped into good citizens and people of strong Christian character.

The Shifler Family Community Center

An investment in the youth of today is also an investment in the future of our community. I am so blessed to have been used by God in this unbelievable way.

Well, there you have it, the story of my life, from my birth up to the present time. In closing, I want to challenge you:

If you have never tried serving God by giving to others, I encourage you to give it a try. I never realized the wonderful life that would follow my simple acts of giving or the joy and blessings that my God would pour out on me. I didn't write this book to tell you how much money I have made, but rather to share how God has blessed me and the pleasure of giving it away. It is so fulfilling and rewarding to be able to meet the needs of others, and it has been a lot of fun. My life has been an amazing journey. That's why I have written this book and why it is entitled *"Now I Know for Sure: You Can't Out-give God!"* All praise, honor, and glory to Him, the Giver of all good gifts!

CPSIA information can be obtained
at www.ICGtesting.com
Printed in the USA
BVHW071235080719
552852BV00017B/371/P